How To Be A Better Catechist
Answers to Questions Catechists Ask Most

Carl J. Pfeifer
Janaan Manternach

Sheed & Ward

Sheed & Ward™ is a service of National Catholic Reporter Publishing
Company, Inc.

Library of Congress Catalog Card Number: 89-61927

ISBN: 1-55612-268-3

Published by: Sheed & Ward
                115 E. Armour Blvd. P.O. Box 419492
                Kansas City, MO 64141-6492

To order, call: (800) 333-7373

*We gratefully dedicate this book
to our first and best
educators in faith,
our parents,
Carl and Emma Pfeifer
Jacob and Anita Manternach*

Contents

Introduction vii

I. Basic Principles

1. What Is Catechesis Anyway? 1
2. What Are We Trying To Accomplish? 4
3. What Are We Supposed To Teach? 8
4. How Can We Get Catechesis to Work? 11
5. How Can We Create a Learning Community? 14
6. How Can We Deal With Human Experience? 17
7. How Can We Get Into The Bible? 20
8. How Can We Relate Classroom and Church? 23
9. What Are the Basic Teachings? 26
10. Whatever Happened to the Saints? 30
11. How Can We Develop Social Concern? 33

II. Overall Strategies

12. How Can We Get Off To A Good Start? 37
13. How Can We Create a Learning Environment? 40
14. How Can We Keep Students Interested? 43
15. How Can We Keep Order So Students Can Learn? 46
16. How Can We Get Through Mid-Year Slump? 49
17. How Can We Use Co-Teachers and Helpers? 52
18. How Can We Involve Parents? 55
19. What Resources Are Available? 58
20. How Can We Make the Most of Summer? 61

III. Practical Tactics

21. Who, Me? Creative? 65
22. How Can We Ask Really Good Questions? 69
23. What About Memorizing? 72
24. How Can We Help Children Learn to Pray? 75
25. How Can We Use Pictures? 78
26. How Can We Use Writing? 81
27. How Can We Use Story and Poetry? 84
28. How Can We Use Music and Song? 87
29. How Can We Use Drawing and Painting? 90
30. How Can We Use Gesture and Movement? 93
31. How Can We Do Service Projects? 96
32. What Have We Learned About Catechesis? 99
Bibliography 102

One day
I would like
to teach,
just a few people,
many and
beautiful things,
that would
help them when
they will
one day teach—
a few people

A Teacher's Prayer

Introduction

We have met thousands of "catechism teachers," "religion teachers" and "catechists" over the past thirty plus years.

We've had the privilege of studying under and working with catechetical experts of several generations and lands.

And we have continued to learn also from the hundreds of children we have taught as volunteer catechists in our own parish and nearby parishes, and from their parents.

All that time catechists have been asking us questions, as we have asked ourselves and others similar questions. Some of these questions keep coming up year after year.

Since 1987 we have been responding to some of the more frequently asked questions in "Catechists' Questions," a regular feature in the monthly newspaper, *The Catechists' Connection*.

Many of the questions and answers in this book have already appeared there. Others may appear in forthcoming issues. All have been re-edited for inclusion in the present book and rearranged in a more logical order both for personal reading and for use in catechist formation or in-service programs.

We hope *How To Be a Better Catechist* will be of help to individual catechists as they face new situations and new questions. The chapters may be read as interest or need suggests. We have tried to be as practical as possible.

This book is a way of thanking the many who have shared their faith and expertise with us. We want to pass on to other catechists what others have so graciously shared with us. To that we add what we have learned through our own successes and failures.

In particular we want to thank Jean-Marie Hiesberger, editor of *The Catechists' Connection,* and her husband, Robert Heyer, managing editor of Sheed & Ward Books, for encouraging us to write the monthly "Catechists' Questions" feature and this book, *How To Be A Better Catechist.*

Carl J. Pfeifer
Janaan Manternach

Arlington, VA
May, 1989

Basic Principles

1
What Is Catechesis Anyway?

"I've been a religion teacher for many years and thought I knew fairly well what I was doing. Last month our new pastor told us we were not religion teachers but catechists. He said that what we do isn't really religious education, but catechesis. What is catechesis anyway?"

Since many people continue to use "religious education" and "catechesis" as synonymns, we would probably be a bit less dogmatic about what you are and what you do than was your new pastor. But he was trying to make a valid and important point.

"Religious education" suggests a *"school model"* of helping people grow in their faith as Catholics. One thinks of teachers, schools, classrooms, textbooks, audio-visuals, tests and homework. It is a familiar model of faith-education with children, youth, and adults.

"Catechesis" at first fails to suggest anything different because it is, for us, a new and strange word. "Catechesis" names a *"Church model"* of helping people mature as believers. Since Vatican II the implications of this "Church model" have become more evident even in the typical parochial school or CCD classroom and curriculum.

Catechesis as Ministry

Following up on the Second Vatican Council, the Vatican's *General Catechetical Directory* described catechesis as an *"ecclesial action,"* an activity of the Church "which leads both communities and individual members of the faithful to maturity of faith" (#21). As such, catechesis is a *"pastoral"* more than an "educational" activity, a *"ministry"* more than a "career" or "job." Its locus is the *parish* or local faith community more than the school or once-a-week religion program.

What does that mean? It means that we "catechists" are involved in continuing the mission of Jesus. Jesus's chief concern was the coming of God's Kingdom—that God's powerful love would transform human hearts and institutions. To facilitate the coming of the Kingdom Jesus *prayed*, he *taught*, he *healed*, and he gathered around him a *community of disciples*. His mission thus came to be seen as that of *priest, prophet*, and *servant-king*.

Today the Church sees the risen Christ continuing these efforts through his disciples in three major Church *ministries—worship, word*, and *service*.

Catechesis is a form of the second of these, the *ministry of the Word*—along with "evangelization" (leading non-believers to believe), "preaching" (within liturgical celebrations), and "theology" (scientific, systematic reflection on God's Word).

As a form of the ministry of the Word *catechesis proclaims and teaches God's Word so believers may grow in their faith.*

As you may be sensing, such an understanding is much richer and more challenging than "teaching the catechism" or "teaching religion," and has greatly influenced how we do "religious education" in the United States.

Catechesis as Ministry of the Word

Seen in this way, as a ministry of the Word within the Church community, catechesis is closely linked with the ministries of worship and service (in which some include the ministry of community-building).

As a result, according to the *National Catechetical Directory* for the United States, catechists have four tasks. *"The fundamental tasks of catechists are to proclaim Christ's message, to participate in efforts to develop community, to lead people to worship and prayer, and to motivate them to serve others"* (#213).

Those four tasks greatly expand the typical idea of classroom teaching, of "teaching religion." They find their natural place within the life of a community of faith, typically the local parish. They imply consciously integrating catechesis with parish worship, with parish social or community-building activities, and with parish service or social action efforts.

In the typical parochial school or once-a-week (CCD) catechetical programs we catechists or (as we are still often called), "religion teachers," need ever to keep in mind these four tasks.

Four Catechetical Tasks

Of the four, *message* is perhaps the most obvious. We are responsible for proclaiming God's Word, incarnated in Jesus Christ, and teaching the basic beliefs and traditions of the Church.

Less obvious, but perhaps more important today than in the past, *community* requires that we work to unite those we teach in a trusting, caring community within the larger Church and world communities.

The third task, *worship,* impels us to do all we can to lead those we catechize to prayer in class and to prayerful lives which include participation in liturgical worship.

Perhaps the most challenging of the four tasks, *service* requires that we inspire and enable those we teach to become more compassionate, reaching out to people who are hurting, and more actively involved in works of social justice and peacemaking.

We hope we have thrown some light on what catechesis is, and deepened your sense of pride in being a "religion teacher," a "catechist," sharing in Christ's own ministry. We will develop these insights as we look further at the goals of catechesis.

2
What Are We Trying To Accomplish?

"I've never taught religion before and I'm wondering what I'm getting into. I feel a bit anxious. I've asked some of my friends who are catechists and they give me different answers. What would I be expected to accomplish as a catechist?"

Becoming a good catechist requires hard work, but it is not an overwhelming task. More and more people like yourself are finding the experience one of the most rewarding of their lives.

Your question gets to the heart of the matter. Church documents since the Second Vatican Council in the early 1960's attempt to spell out just what it is that catechists are to work to accomplish. These documents (see actual quotes on pages 4-5 above) describe the overall goal for catechesis in words like:

A catechist is called to help others grow in their faith as Catholics. The "others" may be children, youth, or adults—individuals or communities.

"Faith" is a person's total response to God and God's Word—embracing the mind, the heart, the spirit, the whole body. Since faith involves the whole personality and how one expresses that faith in actions and lifestyle, we might rephrase our goal in other words.

A catechist is called to help others learn to live Catholic lives.

Such a description is very similar to how parents often describe what they expect their children to get from religion classes, and what they look for themselves in adult religious education programs.

Four Basic Dimensions

We like to break that all-embracing goal down into four major aspects. The four flow from the rich meaning of *"faith"* in the Bible and in Christian tradition.

1. Sharing Catholic Tradition

Catholic faith and lifestyle are colored by some forty centuries of Judaeo-Christian experience. The record and expression of this rich faith heritage is found in the Bible, in worship or liturgy, in official laws and teachings, and in the actual lives of believers. The faith tradition is grounded in human experience and continues to develop as people's experiences expand. Those you catechize have a right to learn elements of this tradition suitable to their age, for example, selected biblical facts and stories, prayers and rituals, ethical and doctrinal teachings, as well as the example of great believers.

In practice you will find the required information in the textbook you will be using. Today's better textbooks spell out exactly what to teach and give detailed practical lesson plans for how to teach it.

2. Discovering Meaning

The traditional content you will be sharing with your students is meant to throw light on their daily experience. Our Catholic tradition is a valuable clue to making sense out of our lives.

The textbooks today are designed to relate biblical stories, liturgical rites, doctrinal teachings, and the stories of saints to students' lives and to contemporary issues. Trust your textbook for the basic process and activities.

Yet be aware that "meaning" is not an abstract formula but a personal perception. As a catechist you best help your students discover life's deeper meaning by sharing something of yourself so they see how the Bible or Catholic teaching or prayer helps you find meaning in your own life.

3. Finding a Way To Live

One of today's greatest challenges for old and young alike is learning to find our way in a complex, exciting, confusing, often frightening world.

Again your textbook gives detailed ways of relating Catholic tradition to contemporary living. But, as with meaning, a creative, happy, faithfilled way of living is learned more from people than from books. Your students may best be drawn to a Catholic way of living by seeing in your life a Christlike way of dealing with people and experiences.

4. Deepening a Relationship

Ultimately discovering life's deeper meaning and finding a faith-filled way of living rest on our relationship with God, whom we meet in Jesus Christ.

So your most basic task as a catechist is to help your students come to know and love Jesus Christ.

Faith is primarily trust, surrender, commitment, love. It is that relationship with God in Christ Jesus that reveals what life is all about and how we are meant to live.

As a catechist you will primarily be sharing with your students your love of Christ, so they may be drawn to know and love him more themselves. You will be sharing with them Someone who is your Friend as well as your Lord. As a banner we love puts it, *"You are the Christ others know best."*

Summary

In terms of priority the four dimensions of faith are reversed from above to (1) *relationship*, (2) *way*, (3) *meaning*, and (4) *tradition*.

An ancient medieval prayer, by St. Richard of Chichester, made popular in the musical *Godspel*, beautifully sums up what catechists are to help people to do:

> *Day by day, day by day,*
> *O dear Lord, three things I pray:*
> * to see thee more clearly,*
> * love thee more dearly,*
> * follow thee more nearly,*
> * day by day.*

3

What Are We Supposed To Teach?

"I honestly think I've been teaching a lot of solid material, but parents and even some of the other teachers say all I'm teaching is 'love, love, love.' They say I'm not teaching any real content. Just what am I supposed to teach?"

Yours is a question we keep hearing from catechists. The answer used to be simple: teach what's in the catechism: the Apostles Creed, the Ten Commandments, the Seven Sacraments and Catholic prayers.

But today even a brief answer to your question is more complicated. Catechetical *content* is much more than what fits in a textbook.

Kinds of Content

For example, in catechesis (as in other teaching-learning experiences) there is *process* content (e.g. praying) and *product* content (e.g. the traditional Catholic prayers). Likewise, there is *affective* content (e.g. trusting, caring) and *cognitive* content (e.g. the story of Abraham's trust, Jesus' example of compassion). And there is *non-verbal* content (e.g. feeling loved) and *verbal* content (e.g. "God is love").

All of these kinds of content are involved in what you are supposed to teach as a catechist. Those you teach learn to pray by praying and seeing you pray as well as by learning treasured Catholic prayers. They learn that "God is love" through your genuine love for them as well as from your quoting the Bible.

Content as God's Word

With that richness in mind we can look more closely at the "content" of catechesis. The *National Catechetical Directory* puts the matter in focus

8

for us: "The source of catechesis, which is also *its content, is one: God's word, fully revealed in Jesus Christ . . .*" (#41).

What we catechists are to teach is, in a word, *God's Word.* Like all content, as we just saw, God's Word is much more than just words.

To teach God's Word implies that we are open to hearing God's Word. Only then can we, as catechists, "echo" that Word.

Where can we hear God's Word? Where is God speaking to us and to our students?

Signs of God's Word

Since the 1950's (earlier in Europe) religious education experts have stressed that God's Word comes to us through "*signs.*" These signs allow us to hear God speaking to us in language we humans can grasp.

Over the years the experts have identified four kinds of signs of God's Word: *natural, biblical, liturgical,* and *ecclesial.* These four signs of God's Word form the rich content of catechesis.

Natural signs

Natural signs of God's Word are all around us. God is with us always and everywhere. The risen Christ graces the totality of human experience. So, an experience like a family meal, a wonder of nature like a butterfly or an earthquake, a political event, like the overthrow of a dictator, a friendly word or touch, a loaf of bread or glass of wine, a scientific, technological marvel like a computer, a beautiful painting or song—everything in human experience may be a sign of God communicating with us. All life is sacramental, every bush may be a "burning bush."

That's why catechetical text books today normally include so much about typical life experiences.

Biblical signs

In a very special way the Bible is God's Word. Through the Bible God speaks to us today as in it we discover how God spoke to others in the past. From the Bible we learn valuable patterns of how God communicates with people. We can learn the dominant themes of God's Word through the centuries. The Bible reveals constants of God's will for human behavior.

So catechesis must have a sizeable biblical content.

Liturgical signs

In personal prayer and communal worship we consciously enter into communication with God. We listen as God's Word is proclaimed and interpreted. We speak, we sing, we act in response to God's Word. The Sacraments celebrate God's Word active in the liturgical assembly and in the whole of life.

Therefore catechetical content embraces the liturgy—Sacraments, traditional prayers, liturgical seasons and feasts, sacramentals.

Ecclesial signs

The term "ecclesial" comes from the Greek and Latin words meaning "church." God speaks through other aspects of the Church's life than through the Bible and liturgy.

The most important of these "ecclesial" signs are (a) *creeds and doctrines,* and (b) *the witness or example of faithful Christians.* God speaks through the Church's official *words,* like the Apostle's Creed, and the teachings of Vatican Council II. And God speaks through the *lives* of great women and men of faith, like the saints.

So the content of catechesis necessarily includes such Church teachings and the lives of saints and other great women and men.

As catechists we are supposed to teach all of the above—natural, biblical, liturgical, and ecclesial signs of God's Word—not all at once, and not just verbally. You seem to have touched the heart of it. Ultimately it *is* all about love.

4

How Can We Get Catechesis To Work?

"I like our new religion books this year. They are so attractive and simple, but my classes don't seem to be working out the way the texts suggest they should. Maybe I don't understand what these new textbooks are getting at. What should I do?"

The new catechetical textbooks are indeed very attractive. Their simplicity flows from the catechetical *process* that they are designed to help you facilitate in your classes. That process is simple but not always easy. Unless you work with that process, your classes may not turn out the way the text suggests.

The Simple Process of Catechesis

The catechetical process is simply *the deliberate relating of your students' life experiences with their Catholic faith tradition.* Or, in the language of the "catechetical signs" (described in the last chapter) it is the *relating of the "natural" signs* (life experience) *with the "biblical," "liturgical" and "ecclesial" signs* (Catholic faith tradition). For example, a lesson on God the Creator might relate the students' own experiences of creativity with the biblical stories of God's creative act.

The process draws on the Catholic belief that God is with us in our day-to-day experiences as well as in our Church with its teachings and rituals. Our experiences open us to a richer understanding and appreciation of the Church's rituals and teachings, which in turn throw light on the deeper meaning of those very experiences.

Your textbook lays out its lesson plans to guide you in making this process happen. The text gives you the key ingredients: a life experience (e.g. "freedom") common to the students you are teaching, and a biblical story (e.g. "exodus"), a liturgical rite (e.g. "baptism"), a doctrinal teaching (e.g. "salvation"), or a saintly life (e.g. "Joan of Arc"), that genuinely relates to that life experience ("freedom").

Making the Process Work

It remains up to you, the catechist, to make the catechetical process work with your students. We have found *four key learning strategies* that facilitate the process in actual practice by engaging the students in the process on a deeper than merely superficial level.

Reflection. Invite and challenge your students to think, dig into, explore, reflect critically on both the life experience and the related aspect of Catholic tradition. Refuse to accept superficial work. Develop your skills at questioning. Single out and affirm more thoughtful, reflective work. Encourage creativity. Expect more from your students than merely parroting back what the textbook says.

Drawing, creative writing, role-playing, dramatizing, open-ended stories, children's literature, evocative photos, good sacred art, popular songs, movies, films, video—all have great potential for helping you and your students to reflect freshly on common experiences in and out of church.

Dialogue. Individual reflection can stimulate sharing or dialogue among you and your students. Dialogue in turn makes possible even richer reflection. Find ways to foster honest sharing among your students and between you and them. Each person's insights can enrich all and the questions of one may trigger questions or answers in others. But little honest sharing can happen unless you work hard at building a sense of mutual understanding and trust in your class.

Given that kind of climate you can encourage genuine sharing with the same kinds of activities we suggested above. One good photo or work of sacred art, for example, can spark a variety of ideas and feelings in the members of your class, enabling a mutually enriching dialogue.

Prayer. Our task as catechists is not only to help our students to know more about life and about God, but to come to know God, to develop a personal relationship with Jesus Christ.

Some form of prayer should be a part of every class. Ideally the prayer will flow out of the lesson's life experience and draw upon the Church's rich prayer tradition.

Prayer may be silent or vocal, individual or communal. Traditional Catholic prayers have a place. So do spontaneous prayers. Students can be helped to pray with photos, sacred art, by writing prayers or hymns, by singing, by using a mantra like the Jesus Prayer, by gesture, dance, processions. The Psalms are a rich source of prayer.

Action. Catechesis is meant to affect how we live. God invites response, commitment, on-going conversion. We teach not a philosophy of life, but a way of living. The action will relate to the area of life experience considered in the lesson as it is illuminated by the related aspect of Catholic faith tradition.

A variety of activities can help students' focus on consequences for their lives, for example, journal writing, creating ads, writing editorials, drawing cartoons, writing resolutions, engaging in service projects or in political actions for justice and peace.

Obviously all such decisions and actions are to be done freely without undue pressures or sanctions.

So, if you trust your textbook and engage your students in these *four key learning strategies,* there is hope that your classes will more and more exhibit the *catechetical process* envisioned in your textbook's lesson plans.

5

How Can We Create a Learning Community?

"I really enjoy being a catechist. I think I've been doing a good job. But something seems missing. Individually my students are great, but they don't seem to want to work together. They are either apathetic or always competing. How can I help them learn more together?"

We are constantly struggling with this ourselves. Our classes tend to reflect the present culture of our country, which values and rewards individual accomplishments in a highly competitive climate.

Catechesis and Community

One of our greatest challenges as catechists is to work to balance the cultural glorification of individual, competitive learning with a more cooperative, collaborative model of community learning.

You may recall that one of the four major tasks we catechists have as ministers of the Word is to *develop community* (see Chapter 1).

The reasons that community-building is so important a part of catechesis are suggested by St. Paul. He writes that we who follow Jesus form "one body" in which the members share "different kinds of spiritual gifts but the same Spirit" (1 Corinthians 12). Individuals are gifted "for building up the body of Christ" (Ephesians 4:12).

God speaks and the Spirit works in each member of the Church—and in each member of our religion classes.

Unless we engage all in the class in the learning-teaching experience, enabling all to share their unique insights and experiences, we may well fail to hear important nuances of God's Word to us all.

14

Building Community

We therefore work hard in our own classes to foster a real sense of community. Here are a few ways we go about building community.

Think "community." Most important is our own attitude. We try to focus on the fact that as teachers we also have much to learn from those we teach, and we all have much to teach each other and to learn from one another. We foster a respect for the surprising potential individuals teaching and learning together have *as a group*.

Get acquainted. We spend a good bit of time the first several classes each year getting to know our students and helping them get to know one another. Learning names is one step. Talking about their favorite people, things, games, TV programs, music, etc., is another.

Leisurely enjoying snacks together is still another. Sometimes we listen to and talk about a favorite rock song. Anything to create a sense of being together, knowing and trusting one another, beginning to care about each other as part of a "community."

During the rest of the year we take a few minutes each class to chat together informally about our recent experiences and current events.

Celebrate and have fun. Fun is a great community builder. We try to celebrate birthdays and other personal accomplishments. We laugh a lot. We build into our classes things the students enjoy, like surprise treats, occasional gifts, a favorite song or game. Thinking about community is an important dimension of planning lessons.

Developing a Learning Community

That human bonding is the key to developing a group that actually *learns and teaches together*—a "teaching-learning community." Here are some ways to encourage collaborative, cooperative learning.

Share results of individual work. Simplest of all, and very important, is letting individuals share their work with the whole group. You may at first have to insist that all listen to one another. Gradually they may come to appreciate each other's gifts. Then honest discussion and cooperation can develop.

Use media. Media have a built-in capacity for fostering community learning. Show the group a photo or painting, for example. All focus on that single object, yet each brings to it a fresh, unique perspective rooted in personal experience, personality, and environment. Together the group's perception is richer than any one member's, and richer than all the members' taken individually. There is a powerful creative energy at work when indivduals really learn together as a group.

Have collaborative projects. Introduce projects or activities that the class can do in small working teams, and as a whole class.

For example, ask the class to create a newspaper for the day Christ died. Pairs or small teams of students work together as editorial writers, cartoonists, headline writers, reporters/interviewers, artists, designers. All assemble the parts to create a newspaper.

Similar collaborative projects might be dramatizing a story, producing a slide-sound show or video tape, making a collage or a mural, putting together a book, writing a song, doing a group sculpture, doing research, or writing a report.

Service projects lend themselves to group planning, execution and evaluation—for example, visiting a nursing home, gathering and taking food to a soup kitchen, organizing a campaign for justice on some school or national issue.

Actually, almost any activity that students usually do alone can also be done by two or more students working together.

The key to developing a teaching-learning community as a catechist is the deep belief in the special power of a community of gifted individuals teaching, learning, and working together.

6
How Can We Deal With Human Experience?

"I don't like the newer religion books because they spend so much time on ordinary, daily experiences. To be honest I get through the life experience part quickly so I have more time to spend on the real content. But I do feel a little guilty doing that. Should I?"

We can't tell you how many times we've heard your question and feelings from other catechists.

You touch on one of the most exciting, yet sometimes disconcerting, aspects of the last twenty-five years of catechetical development.

Most religion textbooks for children and youth, and most adult catechetical approaches, delve into important human experiences as they probe the Scriptures, Church teachings, or Catholic worship.

Why Include Ordinary Experience?

The reason for doing so is that God communicates through daily life as well as through the Church. Pope John XXIII insisted on the need to read the "signs of the times" to discern God's Word. Pope John got the idea and the term, "signs of the times," from Jesus (Matthew 16:3).

Developing Pope John's insight, Vatican II taught that the People of God works to discern *"authentic signs of God's presence and purpose in the happenings, needs, and desires"* experienced by people everywhere (Church in Modern World, 11).

Individuals' experiences, natural phenomena, social and political events, fundamental questions, basic values, contemporary issues—all are part of what the *National Catechetical Directory* calls *"natural signs"* of God's Word, and therefore as much a part of the *content* of catechesis as

17

the "biblical," "liturgical," and "ecclesial" signs of God's Word (see Chapter 3).

To skip, or rush through, the experiential part of catechesis is to short-circuit the *catechetical process* of relating Catholic tradition and daily living (Chapter 4).

How Can We Deal With Life Experience?

Given the importance of human experience in catechesis, we need to find effective ways to help our students explore what is happening in their lives and the lives of people around the world. Here are approaches we have found helpful.

1. Reflect On Your Own Experience

The most important practical step is to deepen your own belief in the traditional Catholic teaching that God is present and communicates with us in the experiences of daily life.

Reflect on where and how you most meet God, on what moments of your life have most influenced your own relationship with God, on how people, job opportunities, accidents, good or bad health have helped you discern God's workings in your life.

2. Build A Trusting Atmosphere

Few people will honestly share their experiences unless they feel respected, trusted, and loved. For your students to share their experiences requires an atmosphere of mutual understanding and trust. Do all you can to build personal relationships between yourself and your students, and between the students.

3. Develop Student-Centered Skills

Our natural tendency as teachers is to talk. We lecture, we explain, we give examples, we exhort. But there is another sort of skills more appropriate to the experiential content of catechesis. Among these are in particular:

Questioning. Good questioning is the key that enables the fruitful sharing of experiences and critical reflection on them. Chapter 22 explores the art of asking good questions in catechesis.

Listening. Careful, sensitive listening—with the heart as well as the ears—has a tremendously liberating power. A person who genuinely listens enables others to become aware of and to share their more meaningful experiences. Good listening picks up feelings and meanings—sometimes not even sensed by the speaker—as well as words. We can learn to "listen" to students' writings, drawings and other creative activities as well as to their spoken words. Few skills are more basic for becoming a more effective catechist.

4. Draw Out Students' Experiences

The most important experiences to explore in your sessions are those of your students.

You can help them surface their experiences through many kinds of activities—e.g. their simply talking about an experience, writing about it, drawing it, acting it out, or expressing it in other art forms.

5. Bring In Others' Experiences

To help student's get at and broaden their experiences, and to reflect on them critically and deeply, share with them similar experiences of others.

Share *your own related experiences* with them. This not only adds to their fund of knowledge but fosters deeper bonds between you.

Poetry and *story* are marvellous resources for illuminating and probing your students experiences.

Photos, paintings and other *art forms, films, videos, popular music,* including rock, are also immensely rich mirrors on personal experience.

So too are the *news media.* Your daily *newspaper,* the *magazines* you subscribe to, contain in each issue reports, stories, editorials, cartoons, photos, ads, that not only expand awareness of events in the world at large but explore common human experiences shared to some degree by your students.

You will find many suggestions for using these kinds of creative activities throughout this book.

7
How Can We Get Into The Bible?

"I know we are supposed to use the Bible more than we used to in teaching religion, but I don't feel too sure of myself. I'm afraid my students will ask me questions. I don't want to misinterpret the Bible. What would you suggest I do?"

Many of us grew up like you with limited knowledge of the Bible. It is natural to feel apprehensive because the Bible is now so central to catechesis, as the official *National Catechetical Directory* states: "Catechesis studies scripture as a source inseparable from the Christian message" (#43). As the "biblical signs" of God's Word, the Sacred Scriptures are an integral part of the content of catechesis.

Fortunately there are many ways and countless resources available to help us become more at home with the Bible. We will suggest one practical approach and several resources. It is important to get directly into the Bible. We suggest that *you start with the actual biblical stories and quotations you will be teaching.* These are found in your textbook. (If you are involved in an adult or children's catechumenate, use the Sunday lectionary.) With the textbook (or lectionary) as your guide, select a biblical passage and follow an approach like this:

(1) *Read the story or quote in your textbook.* Become familiar with it as you will be using it. Notice your response to the story or quote, how it makes you feel, what it says to you. Note any questions you may have about the passage or its use in the lesson.

(2) *Look up the passage in your Bible.* Find that passage in your Bible and read it three times.

(a) *Read it through once.* How does the passage make you feel now? What is it saying to you? Does it differ from what is in your textbook? If so, how? Why?

(b) *Read the passage slowly a second time with a pencil and/or highlighting pen.* Underline words that strike you, note your questions, insights, feelings. Highlight words or verses that particularly touch you, that you would like to make your own.

(c) *Then read the whole chapter of the Bible in which the story or quote is found.* It is important to see it within its *context.* Does this help you better get at the meaning of the passage? Does it answer any of your questions or raise new ones?

As to translations we suggest using the *New American Bible* (with the recently revised New Testament), which is most commonly used in the liturgy and textbooks. Use a *"study edition"* which has helpful notes and references. Study editions are readily available in paperback.

You might prefer the *Jerusalem Bible* because of its more helpful notes and easier reference helps, or the new *Christian Community Bible* because of its more pastoral notes and Third World perspective. Also acceptable are the *Revised Standard Version* or the *New English Bible.*

(3) *Use the helps found in the study edition of the Bible itself.* In front or back of the Bible may be suggestions on "How to Read Your Bible," an overview of biblical history, a "Bible Dictionary," a map of Bible lands, and other general helps. Just before each book of the Bible you will find a brief introduction to that book.

Each page has additional helps. Various versions use different symbols. An "*" or other symbol tells you to look at a footnote for some comment on that particular verse. A small italicized raised letter or other symbol within a verse invites you to look on the page for references to other texts in the Bible which relate to that verse. Following up these references can often throw new light on a passage and show how interrelated are the parts of the Bible.

(4) *Reflect on and pray over the biblical story or quotation.* It is vital to take your new knowledge into yourself and make it your own. This is important for you personally as well as for your teaching.

So spend a few moments with it. Let God's Word become *rooted* in you. Here are some ways to do that:

(a) Try to *imagine what is happening* in the story—the place, the situation, the people, what they are feeling, thinking, saying, doing. What do you feel God saying to you through that text? Through it what is God calling you to do?

(b) Then *talk to God*, to Jesus, to Mary about what you think and feel about God's Word as you hear it in this story or quotation.

(c) *Learn by heart* a phrase or verse you highlighted earlier or that now speaks to you in a special way.

(d) *Decide* how you will try to *live out* what you feel God's Word is calling you to do.

Follow these simple steps with each biblical text you will be teaching— *read* the Bible passage, *study* it, *meditate* on it, *pray* over it, and *decide* from it. That may be enough for you to increase your knowledge of the Bible and your sense of confidence in teaching it.

But you may feel a need to go deeper into the Bible. There are many good books. We would suggest beginning with Jerome Kodell, O.S.B., *The Catholic Bible Study Handbook* (Servant Books, 1985).

We hope these suggestions will help you be *more at home* in God's Word.

8

How Can We Relate Classroom and Church?

"One thing really frustrates me. When I go to Sunday Mass or to a wedding or first communion, I often see some of my students. They are obviously bored. I realize that the liturgy is mostly an adult experience, but is there anything I can do as a catechist to help my students find more meaning in the Mass and sacraments?"

Yours is a common concern of catechists. The relationship of catechesis and liturgy is vital, but often remains unrealized in reality.

You may remember that the "liturgical signs" are an important part of catechetical content (Chapter 3), and that one of the catechist's four basic tasks is to "lead people to worship and prayer" (see Chapter 1).

The *National Catechetical Directory*, states that "from its earliest days the Church has recognized that liturgy and catechesis support one another" (#36). But this mutual support does not usually happen by accident. It takes work.

There are many practical things you can do in your classes to help your students better understand the liturgy and perhaps be more motivated to participate in it.

The *NCD* indicates that catechesis "prepares people for full and active participation in liturgy (by helping them understand its nature, rituals, and symbols) and at the same time flows from liturgy, inasmuch as, reflecting upon the community's experiences of worship, it seeks to relate them to daily life and to growth in faith" (#113).

The catechist's tasks are therefore carried out *before* and *after* liturgical celebrations.

Catechesis, Liturgy, Daily Life

Our experience suggests that the heart of such liturgical catechesis lies in four areas:

Christian attitudes. The *NCD* (#36) urges catechists to help students become more prayerful, thankful, repentant, confident and open to others in daily life. These basic human, Christian attitudes are the inner "stuff" of liturgy.

Without some human feeling of gratitude, for example, the eucharistic celebration will be missing its heart. Without genuine repentance there simply is no sacrament of reconciliation.

So we catechists need to nurture these attitudes in our students as the necessary soil or groundwork for liturgy. We do this more by our own example than by exhortation.

Sensitivity to symbols. Just as important is the need to open students to the whole world of symbol. Liturgy is made up of symbolic actions and things: sharing food, anointing with oil, exchanging rings.

Yet our students live in a world and in schools that value science, mathematics, computer literacy—what can be experimented with, measured, bought and sold—more than imagination, poetry, art, story, rituals, and symbols.

So it often falls to catechists to exercise their students in creative, imaginative, poetic, dramatic experiences. Without such sensitivity the symbolic language of liturgy may remain unintelligible to them.

Actually, all catechesis is to be, as James Dunning claims, "full of symbol and story, wonder and prayerfulness, silence and mystery, imagination and appreciation—*just as is liturgy.*"

Bible background. Liturgical symbolism rests on biblical stories and images as well as on natural symbolism. For example, the use of water in baptism draws on the natural symbolism of water as cleansing, refreshing, life-giving and death-dealing. But the baptismal waters draw still richer meaning from the biblical stories centering on water, for example, the stories of creation, flood, exodus, crossing the Jordan river into Canaan.

Knowing the bible stories and their meaning is essential to fuller appreciation of the liturgical rites. Catechists have the privilege of engaging their students with these rich biblical stories.

Linking liturgy and catechesis. You can do much to more explicitly link your classes to your students' experience in the liturgy.

Some catechists integrate the two, building their entire catechesis around the *Lectionary.* Lectionary catechesis is characteristic of catechumenates for adults and children.

Others bring into their classes liturgical elements like:

Liturgical seasons. Foster awareness of liturgical seasons in your lessons, not just by mentioning that it is, for example, Advent, but also by using Advent colors, art of Advent Bible stories, popular songs or photos suggestive of waiting and expectation.

Liturgical prayers. Incorporate into your classes appropriate prayers from the *Missal* or *Sacramentary* or *Liturgy of the Hours.* Many of them fit perfectly the lessons in your textbook.

Liturgical hymns/songs. Just using hymns your students sing at Mass on Sundays helps bridge class room and church. Draw from the hymn book your parish uses most.

Liturgical symbols/rituals. Some of the gestures, movements, and physical objects used symbolically in the liturgy can fit well into many of your lessons.

Consciously linking elements of liturgy and catechesis is not difficult once you sense its value.

Good luck in your efforts to help your students grow in appreciation of the Church's liturgy.

9

What Are the Basic Teachings?

"The pastor and some parents in our parish keep insisting that we religion teachers emphasize 'the basic teachings,' or 'catholic doctrine and morality.' Why are they so up-tight about doctrine? I'm not always sure myself anymore what the Church teaches. What are the 'basic teachings'?"

In a time of rapid change and confusion such as we have been experiencing, believers understandably look to their Church for clear, stable truths—something to hold on to.

Also, "doctrine" is a vital dimension of the content of catechesis, one of the *ecclesial signs* of God's Word (see Chapter 3). Doctrine is the Church's official interpretation of its experience of Christ. Catechists need to be concerned about teaching doctrine.

Concern about doctrine arose early in the Church's history. Christians, experiencing massive change and mass conversions, soon formulated basic statements of what Christians believe. We know their summaries of "basic teachings" as the *Apostles' Creed,* and the *Nicene Creed* (recited each Sunday at Mass).

In a sense those two traditional Creeds remain our best brief statements of Catholic doctrine.

But people normally want more detail and interpretation. So in 1978 the Bishops of our country included a summary of the "Principal Elements of the Christian Message for Catechesis," as Chapter V of the *National Catechetical Directory.*

Basic Teachings

Here is the outline of that official summary of basic Catholic teachings. As you read through the list, compare it with the Apostle's Creed and Nicene Creed.

> *The Mystery of the One God*
> *Creation*
> *Jesus Christ*
> *The Holy Spirit*
> *The Church*
> *The Sacraments*
> *The Life of Grace*
> *The Moral Life*
> *Mary and the Saints*
> *Death, Judgment, Eternity*

There is no space here to elaborate on the rich synthesis of which this is but an outline. You may find it helpful to read the actual text in the *NCD*.

Of all the Church's doctrines, the *NCD* groups the *most basic* of basic teachings under four headings:

• ". . .the *mystery of God* the Father, the Son, and the Holy Spirit, Creator of all things;

• the *mystery of Christ* the incarnate Word, who was born of the Virgin Mary, and who suffered, died, and rose for our salvation;

• the *mystery of the Holy Spirit,* who is present in the Church, sanctifying it and guiding it until the glorious coming of Christ, our Savior and Judge;

• and the *mystery of the Church,* which is Christ's Mystical Body, in which the Virgin Mary holds the pre-eminent place." (47).

How Should We Teach Basic Doctrines?

Knowing the basic teachings is one thing. Teaching doctrine well in catechesis is another. Both Rome's *General Catechetical Directory* (37-46) and the *NCD* (47) make some important observations about how to teach Catholic doctrine. Neglecting these criteria can lead to distorting the basic teachings.

(1) Catechesis is *trinitarian* and *christocentric*. It emphasizes the one God, Father, Son and Holy Spirit, and centers on Jesus Christ. We need to keep central what is truly at the center of Catholic teaching, and not make secondary doctrines central.

(2) Catechists need to present the Christian message *as an organic whole*, in such a way that the *inter-relationships* of the various elements are clear. This prevents us from exaggerating or isolating one or other doctrine.

(3) We need to recognize a *hierarchy of truths*, namely that some teachings are more important than others. Not all doctrines have equal priority. Our catechesis needs to respect that hierarchy or order of importance.

(4) In teaching the basic truths we need to *keep in touch* with the other important forms of life in the Church community (social, institutional, liturgical, theological, artistic, activist). Doctrine is also to be taught and understood in relationship to the Bible and other forms of Christian tradition.

(5) Catechists must always relate the basic truths to the *realities of human existence*, always keeping in mind *the cultural, linguistic, and other* circumstances of the learners. In this way we assure that doctrine is not divorced from people's real lives, and that doctrinal language remains intelligible to our hearers.

(6) Catechesis must respect the *historical character* of God's saving Word. We need to keep in mind the *memory of the past, awareness of the present, and hope of future life*. This keeps us from viewing doctrine as overly static and closed to development and further insights.

(7) Catechesis must be carried out *under the guidance of the magisterium of the Church* so that we avoid presenting personal biases as Church teachings.

(8) Catechesis must make use of the *best contemporary methodologies* in presenting Catholic doctrine. Just explaining, memorizing or repeating orthodox words, is not an adequate doctrinal catechesis.

We hope this helps you better to grasp the importance of "basic teachings," and to teach doctrine more faithfully.

Fortunately the authors and publishers of catechetical textbooks do much to help you by following the official catechetical guidelines.

10

Whatever Happened to the Saints?

"When I grew up, we learned about a lot of saints. I still remember St. Tarcisius and St. Christopher. I don't hear much about them anymore. Should I do much with saints in my religion classes? Where can I find help for teaching about saints?"

Catholic attitudes to saints (including Mary) have changed rather dramatically over the past years, as your letter suggests. You are not the only one puzzled by this.

The loss of interest in saints during the 60's and 70's was due to a variety of causes, for example: the Vatican Council emphasized the central place of Jesus Christ in the life and worship of Christians; Catholics turned more to the Bible and the liturgy than to previously popular devotions; some stories of saints were found to lack solid historical evidence.

In the last several years we have been experiencing a revival of interest in exemplary Christians as models for ourselves and our children. The *National Catechetical Directory* recognizes the witness of exemplary Christians as one of the *"ecclesial signs"* of God's self-comunication in the world, and a vital part of catechetical *content.* "The lives of heroic Christians, the saints of past and present, show how people are transformed when they come to know Jesus Christ in the Spirit" (45).

This renewed awareness of the importance of saints in catechesis is evident in most of the newer religion textbooks and in the many recent books about saints.

Make the Most of Saints and Heroes

So, to answer your first question: Yes, include saints and other great human beings, living and dead, in your religion classes. They provide us and our students with real-life examples of what it means to live as followers of Jesus and as admirable human persons.

Practical Ways to Teach About Saints

In response to your second question, here are some approaches we have found helpful.

Explore students' names. Most Catholics are named after a saint or other hero. Have your students find out more about the saint whose name they bear. As a class, take a moment to celebrate each youngster's "name day" on or near the feast of the patron or patroness.

Have the students look into the patron saints of the jobs or professions members of their families engage in. For example, St. Martin de Porres is patron of hairdressers.

Helpful resources include John J. Delaney, *Dictionary of Saints* (Garden City, NY: Doubleday, 1980).

Follow the liturgical calendar. The Church honors one or several saints on most days of the year. Use a missal, missalette, or liturgical calendar to guide you. Take a moment in class to recall and pray to the saint(s) of the day. Helpful resources include *Saint of the Day,* ed. Leonard Foley, O.F.M. (Cincinnati: St. Anthony Messenger, 1974); Butler's *Lives of the Saints,* Concise Edition, ed. Michael Walsh (San Francisco, Harper & Row, 1985).

Some calendars include saints, and other great men and women who may not be included in the liturgical calendar but whose lives have special significance in the light of contemporary challenges. See, for example, *Calendar of Holy Women* (Bear & Company, Drawer 2860, Santa Fe, NM 87501); *Calendario de la Familia Catolica* (J.S. Paluch Company, Division Nacional para las Vocaciones, 3825 N. Willow Road, P.O. Box 1931, Schiller Park, IL 60176); *Josephite Black Arts Calendar* (Josephite Pastoral Center, 1200 Varnum Street, N.E., Washington, DC 20017); HCA Classroom Calendar (Holy Childhood Association, 1720 Massachusetts Avenue, NW, Washington, DC 20036).

You might also find helpful Boniface Hanley, O.F.M., *Ten Christians* (1979), and *No Strangers to Violence, No Strangers to Love* (1983), both by Ave Maria Press.

Creatively Explore Saints' Lives. Use a variety of creative approaches to bring the lives of saints into your students' lives—e.g. prayer, poetry, art, puzzles, drama, maps, film, filmstrips, video. Helpful resources include Janaan Manternach & Carl Pfeifer, *People to Remember* (New York: Paulist Press, 1987); Janice Gudeman, *Creative Encounters with Creative People* (Carthage, IL: Good Apple, 1984); monthly issues of popular catechetical magazines.

Make the Most of News Media. Not all saints are dead and canonized. The daily newspaper, TV news, as well as magazines of all kinds, frequently have stories of exemplary persons. The July 6, 1987 *Newsweek*, for example, carried a lengthy cover story, "A Celebration of Heroes," which included 51 brief sketches of contemporary American heroes in all walks of life.

Share such news stories with the students. Ask them to explore the story in relation to their own lives. You can make up simple work sheets with several pointed questions, or ask them to write what most strikes them about the person whose story you shared with them.

Many diocesan newspapers each week carry a short life of a great Christian, for example, Janaan Manternach's weekly *Children's Story Hour*, syndicated by the National Catholic News Service.

Make Personal Saint Books. Have your students build their own books of saints and other heroes as the year goes on. Encourage them to draw on any resources available to them—including the example of family members, relatives, neighbors, friends and other people they may actually know whose lives they find admirable and attractive.

11
How Can We Develop Social Concern?

"I keep hearing about the Church's concern for justice and peace. This was never a big part of my Catholic education. As a catechist I feel I should be doing more about educating my students to a greater social concern. But I really don't know what to do. Any ideas?"

In recent years, like you, we have also come to realize how important a part of catechesis is education for justice and peace.

The *National Catechetical Directory*, devoting an entire chapter (VII) to "Catechesis for Social Ministry," sees *"taking part in Christian service"* as one of the four *content* components of catechesis (#39), and one of the four *tasks* of catechists (210) [see Chapters 1, 3].

But how to do that task?

Educating for Justice and Peace

Perhaps the first step we catechists can take is to become more socially aware and committed. We might do ourselves the things we plan to do with our students.

Fostering Needed Attitudes. Our efforts at educating for justice and peace begin with the kinds of attitudes we foster right in our classes. We need to work at creating a just and peaceful class atmosphere in which our students may learn to appreciate the values of respect, compassion, justice and peace by experiencing them. Our example is the key factor.

(a) *Fostering self-esteem.* Catholic social teaching centers on belief in the dignity of each person, created in God's image. We can help our students sense their own worth and gifts by nurturing their self-esteem in many simple ways, like affirming students and their abilities, listening to them, and treating them with respect.

(b) *Fostering respect for others.* Since each person has the same basic dignity and rights, we need to help our students grow in respect for others—by how we treat each of them and expect them to treat us, how we help them listen to one another and observe basic class rules so all are able to learn, how we refuse to tolerate violence.

(c) *Fostering compassion and caring.* The heart of education for justice and peace is helping our students *feel for* and *with* others, particularly with those who are in any way hurting or in need. We can begin fostering compassion within the circle of students themselves. How many of our students suffer from divorces, loneliness, their own or a family member's illness or injury, the death of a pet or loved one?

(d) *Fostering collaboration.* So much of contemporary life and education fosters competition. A degree of competitiveness is healthy, but needs to be balanced by a strong sense of collaboration. We can engage our students in collaborative activities and projects, requiring them to work together.

Engaging in Christian social analysis. In addition to fostering these and similar attitudes we can involve our students in a process of Christian *social analysis*, adapting it to our students' age and readiness and to the lessons in our textbooks.

Here are the four steps of the process, which can be used with any issue, e.g. poverty, hunger, homelessness, discrimination, etc.

(a) *Seeing.* The process begins with a hard look at the reality at issue, ideally through actual contact with the victims, people who are suffering injustice. It may be by a direct personal experience like visiting a soup kitchen, or by less direct contact through the news media, photographs, a filmstrip, film or video, poetry, story, or simulation games. This step must involve a look that moves the feelings and touches the heart.

(b) *Analyzing.* Then we guide the students to ask "Why?" Why are so many hungry? Why are so many poor in so rich a country? Why do women make less money than men?

This is the time for gathering more data, for thinking, for critical reflection, for drawing upon experts. Always probing: "Why?" What are the causes? Who is hurting? Who may be benefitting?

(c) *Judging.* The next step brings the Gospel message and Catholic social teaching to bear on the realities uncovered in the first two steps. Sources for the Church's social teaching include, for example, biblical stories or quotations, stories of saints, liturgical prayers, excerpts from social encyclicals or pastorals.

In this step the students are to discover how contrary to God's plan is the unjust reality they looked at and analyzed, and to sense Christ's call to do something to right this injustice.

(d) *Acting.* The process leads to decisions and actions to help the victims and to change the unjust structures causing their pain. The actions could begin with *prayer* right during class.

Social actions include *compassionate help* to hurting persons, like raising money, gathering food or clothes, visiting a nursing home, and actions, ranging from writing letters to engaging in public demonstrations aimed at *systemic change* of unjust systems, institutions and structures that cause hurt.

In these ways we may help our students grow in their commitment to social justice, which Peter Henriot defines as "*loving people so much that we work to change structures that violate their dignity.*"

Overall Strategies

12
How Can We Get Off To A Good Start?

"I'm not very organized. Some years I've run out of ideas before the year is half over. Many times I think of just the perfect story or film after a class is over. Much of the time I don't feel I really know where I'm going. Can you help me?"

We've had the same experience at times. So have many catechists we have known. From our own painful experiences and those of other catechists we have discovered a few helpful tips on *planning* at the start of the year. Here are some of them.

1. Look at a calendar. Look carefully at an ordinary year-long calendar that covers the period of time you will be teaching.

 • Mark the date of each scheduled class with a bright color.

 • Count them up to see exactly how many sessions you will have.

 • Mark with another bright color any holydays, holidays, seasons, or other important dates that are near your class dates.

2. Look at the Church Calendar. If at all possible get a calendar from your principal or DRE that has the major religious events that will be celebrated in your parish during the period when you will be teaching. The parish calendar should include important liturgical feasts, seasons, and holydays, as well as major parish events like First Communion, Confirmation, parish social events, parish social action projects.

• Mark these important events on your *main calendar,* the one that you have been marking so far.

3. Look at your textbook. Turn to the Table of Contents of your text book. Study it to see:

• how many chapters or lessons there are; compare this with the number of classes you have.

• how many of the lesson topics tie into the events you have marked on your calendar; jot down these events with their dates beside the titles of related lessons in the Table of Contents.

• which lessons seem at this early stage to be most easily omitted (if the text has more lessons than you have classes), or to deserve more time (if you have more classes than the textbook has lessons), or which other lessons might replace or be added to what is in the textbook.

4. Make a Working Schedule. On the basis of what you have done so far, draw up a schedule that best relates the lessons of your textbook to what you see will be happening during the period you will be teaching. For example, feel free to move a lesson on the Holy Spirit or Confirmation from its logical place in the text to its more meaningful place for your students in relation to the parish celebration of Confirmation.

Now you have a reasonable idea of *when* you will be teaching *what* the rest of the year.

5. Get to Know Your Textbook. Your guide and companion all year will be your textbook. So it makes sense to get well acquainted as early as possible. Set aside a quiet hour and

• refresh your memory of the Table of Contents.

• read the Introduction (which may be in the front or the back) to get a sense of the makeup of your particular textbook and the reasons why it is put together the way it is.

• notice particular features of your text that may be helpful as the year progresses, like prayers, maps, lists of films, children's books.

• read carefully one lesson that most insterests you; begin with the pupil's book; then study the teacher's manual for that same lesson; then look at any other related materials your textbook program includes for that lesson, like worksheets, filmstrips, parents' notes.

6. Make a Personal Resource File. Now that you are familiar with your schedule and your textbook, you can greatly enrich your teaching by making a personal resource file. Use an empty drawer, or set up a simple file, with sections for each Unit or each Lesson you will be teaching.

Then as life goes on you will more than likely notice in newspapers or magazines you normally read stories, photos, art, ads, cartoons and headlines that fit one or other of your lessons. You may notice similarly useful items in stores, on TV, in conversations, or in your own experience. Just toss your discoveries in your drawer or file them in your file. When you come to prepare a given lesson, you may already have in your personal resource file an excellent picture, story, or real-life example to add interest and vitality to your class.

Without a place to put things you find as the year goes on, you will not notice the wealth of resources all around you until it is too late for use in a lesson.

All of this planning may take a total of two or three hours. The effort will simplify and enrich your more detailed planning for each lesson as the year goes on. The time and anxiety it will save you during the year is many times more than that initial investment of time. You will feel more confident and your students will benefit from your more creative and interesting classes.

13

How Can We Create a Learning Environment?

"I have to teach my CCD class in a classroom. I feel the children dislike being in a classroom again. Is there anything I can do about it?"

"I'm having my religion classes in my home for the first time, and am not sure what room to use."

"I'm really frustrated! How can you have a religion class in an office or a library? That's what they want me to do this year!"

We will attempt to respond to these three questions together. All three relate to the *space* or *environment* that is best for catechesis.

In one sense the place where we teach is secondary. Catechesis depends more on personal relationships than on spatial arrangements.

It is possible to be an effective catechist in almost any place.

Yet there is no question that the physical space where we have our religion classes may greatly help or hinder our teaching and our students' learning.

We learned this almost accidentally some years ago. We were substituting for a catechist whose lesson was on prayer. The room was the school cafeteria. We adults were seated at long cafeteria tables. It was uncomfortable. We could not see those on the same side of the table we were seated on. We had to strain to hear. Nothing much happened. No one shared. No one prayed.

So we changed the environment. We found some folding chairs, and arranged them in a circle. People began to share how they prayed. We all learned a great deal about prayer. Then we prayed, individually, together.

All that changed was the space, the arrangement, the environment.

A Caring Environment

What is vital is that the place in which we teach *be* and *communicate* an environment of *care* and *respect*. Someone used the term, *an environment of grace.*

That means that when you and the students gather—or when parents or observers visit—all *sense,* just from the appearance and arrangement of the room, your *care* and *respect*: for yourself, for your students, for what you are teaching and learning together, and for the material things being used.

To become aware of the potential your place for catechesis has to become a caring environment, visit it by yourself sometime. Walk around, sit down, look around, listen.

How do you feel there? Welcome? Happy? Closed in? Eager to get out? Hot? Cold? Comfortable? Eager to learn?

Try to discover what it is about the space that makes you feel the way you do. Explore how you can capitalize on features that encourage positive feelings, and minimize those that create negative feelings.

What are the best features of the space for your purposes?

What aspects of the place seem least conducive to learning together?

As you reflect on how the space makes you feel, begin noticing details in relation to you, your students, and the teaching-learning process. Your attention to physical details reveals to your students without any words your respect and care for them and for what you are learning together. For example:

Is the size of the room suitable to the number and age of your students? If it is too large, you can creatively set off a part of it for your class. For younger children you may need more space per child because of their need to move about and be more involved physically. In any class you will want to have enough space to allow for a variety of kinds of activities. If you cannot move from a too small room, consider how you might do some activities outside the room.

Is the furniture suitable? Fixed desks are less suitable than moveable ones. Sofas or chairs that are too comfortable may interfere with active learning. If you can move chairs, tables or desks, consider different arrangements for various activities. If you cannot move anything, explore ways in which the students can move about. Consider the use of carpet remnants, and/or pillows, to make the floor itself more useable.

Can all see and hear one another easily? Be sure the arrangement allows for easy communication. Find ways to minimize outside, distracting noises. Arrangements that are more circular are usually more effective than fixed rows one behind the other.

Will you be able to use various media, like slides, filmstrips, films, video? Can the lighting be controlled so the room may be darkened? Where can you set up the needed equipment?

How can you make the space more attractive, exciting, beautiful? Explore how you might more effectively control the amount and quality of light. Perhaps music at appropriate moments would create an atmosphere of reflection, prayer or creativity. Decide where you can place beautiful photos or paintings related to your lesson. Where might you display the creative work of the students or have an attractive, instructive bulletin board?

Do all you can to make the room attractive to the senses. Needless to say, be sure the room is clean and carefully arranged.

The space in which we work as catechists can have a sacramental quality, revealing and making present to our students God's grace and our care. A classroom, office, or room in your home can become a creative learning environment, an "environment of grace."

14

How Can We Keep Students Interested?

"How do you hold students' interest? Things go well for the first few minutes. But no matter how hard I try, the kids quickly lose interest. I feel excited about what I'm telling them, but they quickly get bored. It's so frustrating. What can I do?"

Yours is one of the questions we hear most often from catechists. Many parents echo the same concern when they tell us their youngsters complain that religion class is boring.

In order to find ways to make your classes more interesting to your students, it may be helpful to reflect for a moment on how you yourself learn. Chances are your students learn in similar ways. Ask yourself this question: *"How and what do I learn best?"* Jot down your answers.

If you are honest, you may discover that you best learn what you want to learn, what you need to learn, what relates to your daily experience, what is important to you, what you are ready to learn.

You may also notice how you learn best: through experience, observing others, sharing with others, through stories, pictures, concrete examples, doing things, making mistakes, being involved. You may find that the words of an ancient Chinese sage reflect your own learning experience:

"What I hear, I forget.
What I see, I remember.
What I do, I understand."

If those you teach are like you, they quickly become bored with extended periods of listening to your words, no matter how meaningful those words are to you and no matter how well you have prepared your presentation. The key to engaging and holding their interest is to adapt your teaching to their learning. Here are a few tips we have learned.

1. The less you talk, the more they may learn. Most of us teachers spend most of our class time talking. It can take a real effort, and a fearful act of faith, deliberately to stop talking. But that may be the first step in increasing student interest and learning.

2. The more the students do, the more you will teach them. This may seem paradoxical, but the effectiveness of your teaching will improve as you turn the responsibility for learning back to your students. Your task becomes that of planning meaningful activities and facilitating student involvement in them.

Actually this is more challenging than preparing and delivering a good lecture. Naturally you will also speak—interpreting, explaining, answering questions, and more important, asking questions.

As you prepare your lesson, ask yourself how your students can learn what you are to teach in creative ways that involve them in *eyes-on activities* (e.g. photos, art, maps, cartoons, newspapers, magazines, filmstrips, films, video), *hands-on activities* (e.g. drawing, writing, painting, arts and crafts, collage, posters, banners, movement, gesture, dance, drama, role-plaing, games), and *ears-on activities* (e.g. stories, poetry, music, song, silence, discussion, lecture, debate).

3. Stay close to their experience. No matter how excited you may feel about a religious fact or truth, your students cannot sustain interest in it unless it relates to their own lives. Most of the modern religion texts begin every lesson with some experience from the world of the students. This is not just good pedagogy; it is good theology.

Not only do we normally only learn what relates to our lives, but God's presence and God's Word are found in our own experience as well as in the traditional sources of bible, liturgy, doctrine and the example of other believers.

It is vital that we catechists make every effort to know our students and the world of their experience. This is particularly difficult in once-a-week settings. The students' creative work is a most valuable source of discovering what they are like, what their interests, values, questions, and problems are. The less you talk and the more they are purposefully active, the more you will come to know them and their world.

4. Stay on course. The increased activity of the students can lead to confusion and distraction unless you are clear from the start about the goal or objectives of the lesson. You and the students need to have a sense that what everyone is doing is purposeful, that one step follows from and leads to another. This is one of the most important steps in planning your classes. Keep your plan simple, with one major theme, and with activities that move step-by-step toward a single goal. It is not a matter of many activities, but of one or several carefully selected meaningful activities.

5. Keep things moving. We all, and today's young people perhaps even more, learn more when we sense that things are moving. Attention span is much shorter than we often think. It is vital for learning that there be a change of pace and rhythm suitable to the students' age level and development.

To sum up: Try to make your classes more "student-centered" and less "teacher-centered." Chances are good that this will greatly increase student interest.

15

How Can We Keep Order So Students Can Learn?

"Here's my problem. I seem to spend much of my class time trying to get enough order to teach at least a few minutes. I'm not a trained teacher. I'm frustrated and feel there must be something I'm missing. Could you give me some ideas about improving discipline?"

We've been teaching many years, but find discipline a continual challenge, especially in the once-a-week religious education setting.

Class discipline is important, but it is not an end in itself. It has a purpose, namely that you and your students are able to interact in ways that allow them to learn. The final test of effective discipline is whether your students are learning. Good discipline may look and sound quite different in other classes with other teachers.

With that in mind, let's look at our "Ten Commandments of Good Discipline."

1. Respect yourself. You are a teacher, an educator, a catechist. That is something very special—whether you are trained or not. Few tasks in society are as important as teaching, few ministries in the Church as important as catechesis.

And, remember, your students' respect for you hinges greatly on how you respect yourself.

Some important signs of your self-respect as a catechist show up in how you dress for class, how you expect your students to address you and act in your presence, the care you put into preparing your lessons and the classroom environment.

2. Respect your students. Discipline is less a function of power than of respect. Effective discipline is ultimately self-discipline, which arises from respect for the rights and needs of all. It is important that we teachers model the kind of respect for others that we expect from our students.

Your respect for your students shows in how much you try to get to know them, how carefully you listen to and remember what they say, how you try to adapt to their differing learning styles, how carefully you prepare, and how you review and respond to their creative work.

3. Trust your students. Perhaps the ultimate sign of respect for those you teach is to trust them.

Convey a mistrust of individuals or of the class and you cut away the deeper motivations of the students to learn and to act responsibly. Expecting the worst inevitably assures the worst.

Students sense your trust when you clearly expect them to learn. Allow them to take responsibility for their learning, suggest alternative approaches and be creative.

4. Work hard to teach well. Good teaching facilitates good discipline.

If your students are bored, passive, uninterested and uninvolved, discipline problems can be predicted. If they are actively involved in learning something that touches their lives, you should have fewer discipline problems.

Critically important is your careful preparation of your classroom and lesson plan, familiarity with the content and methodologies of your text, awareness of your goals, and your on-going efforts to improve your teaching skills.

5. Reinforce good behavior. Praise and appreciation are powerful motivators. Affirmation nurtures self-respect and self-discipline. Affirm your students as often as possible, but always honestly—for their efforts as well as their accomplishments, and most of all, just for being who they are. You can affirm with sincere words, with the giving of added trust and responsibility, with awards, with a hug.

6. Condemn bad behavior, but not the person who misbehaves. By contrast be careful to distinguish between disruptive actions and the person doing them. Condemn the specific action but never the person. A way of doing this is to use "I" messages. Instead of saying *"You* are making me angry," try *"I* am getting upset by your constant whispering." This allows the student to sense that you are not rejecting him or her as bad when you reject his or her actions.

7. Avoid threats and put-downs. Power tactics like threats, put-downs, intimidation, ridicule, punishment, may induce a certain amount of external compliance, but tend to undermine the inner respect that enables true discipline. A silent pause is often much more effective than shouting.

8. Teach needed skills. Students may lack bacic communications and social skills. They may never have learned how to listen to directions, to work cooperatively, to be silent, to resolve conflicts, to be polite, to set or respect time limits. Help them learn these necessary skills.

9. Have a few simple, clear rules that are consistently enforced. Most groups, even of adults, need some rules to ensure order and the pursuit of their goals. Classroom rules should be as few as possible, only as many as required to ensure learning. We normally invite our students to suggest the rules they feel are vital if all are to be able to learn. A few basic rules may be needed, but effective discipline rests more on your relationship with the students than on rules.

10. Cultivate a sense of humor, tolerance and flexibility. No matter how well you teach and how good your students are, there will inevitably arise disciplinary situations that are best handled with a good laugh and an understanding of human weakness and unpredictability.

16
How Can We Get Through Mid-Year Slump?

"I seem to have the 'blahs.' So do my students. It may be the time of year—cold, grey winter. Or maybe we're just bored. Whatever the reason, the earlier excitement has definitely cooled. How can we break this slump? What can I do to spark up myself and my classes?"

We usually feel about the same way you do by the time February arrives. There is a natural letdown after the Christmas high. In many parts of the country the climate contributes to a cooling of enthusiasm. Catechists and students have settled into fairly predictable patterns by now. A mid-season slump is not surprising. But the "blahs" need not be terminal.

Here are a few steps we have found helpful to rekindle our own and our students' interest.

1. Have a Slump Celebration. Some years ago catechist Gladys Busch, C.S.C., described how she and her catechists renewed their own spirits during the mid-Winter slump. They planned and then enjoyed an evening of praying and partying together.

The "Slump Celebration" began with a specially designed Eucharistic liturgy. The catechists selected readings, songs, prayers and symbols that celebrated life. All participated actively in the celebration.

After Mass they gathered informally to get to know one another better and to share experiences and ideas about their teaching. A warm candle-light atmosphere encouraged relaxed sharing. Large "slump-people" cutouts decorated the walls with a touch of humor. Wines and cheeses, fruit and coffee, added to the festivity.

Many parishes have found similar "Slump Celebrations" a great way to foster community among catechists and to drive out mid-winter "blahs."

2. Recharge Yourself. Even if your parish does not provide an opportunity for its catechists to recharge their slumping spirits, you can take some helpful steps yourself. Some catechists make time to attend a catechetical workshop or lecture. Others renew their spirits by reading a book, viewing a video, or listening to a cassette recording about some aspect of teaching religion. Still others find a weekend retreat experience best suits their needs.

What is important is that you take some concrete step to enrich your understanding, develop your skills and renew your enthusiasm. Then you will be better equipped to help your students out of their slump.

3. Change Your Pace. Every relationship runs the risk of too much routine. From time to time you and your students need a a bit of surprise, a break in familiar patterns. Here are a few change-of-pace suggestions we have found helpful.

a. *Field Trip.* A carefully planned trip away from the normal class setting can spark renewed interest. Such a trip should relate clearly to what you are teaching. For example, we have found a tour of the parish church very interesting for young children studying "church" or "sacraments." Older youngsters may find a visit to the diocesan cathedral or to a local shrine a fresh way to grasp the meaning of "bishop," "diocese," or "saint." Almost any age child may find a visit to an art gallery or museum helpful for appreciating biblical stories and the life and teachings of Jesus. Most Catholic youngsters find a guided visit to a Protestant church, Jewish synagogue, Muslim mosque, or other place of worship a fascinating way to deepen their own Catholic identity while coming to respect the faith of others.

b. *Guest Speaker.* A new face about this time of year can bring added interest to your students. With a little thought you should be able to find someone in your parish, neighborhood or city who is both competent and willing to share with your class.

One of our most successful 8th grade classes one year was on the topic of monasticism. We invited a young Benedictine to share with our students what it meant to him to be a monk. The year before, we invited a parishioner who was a drama teacher to work with our 3rd graders in acting out an appropriate child's story.

Every parish has women and men with talent and experience in a wide variety of fields. Their sharing with the students can bring a valuable "real-life" dimension to your religion class, as well as spark renewed interest during slump times.

c. *Class Mass.* We have found few experiences as meaningful as a special Eucharistic liturgy for our students and their parents. The students enjoy and learn from planning and preparing the celebration.

The actual liturgical experience brings together priest, parents, catechist, and students in a common expression of faith. Refreshments after the Eucharist provide an informal opportunity to become better acquainted with the parents of your students. Sometimes observing a student with his or her father or mother can help you better understand that child.

There are many other ways of bridging the mid-winter slump—for example, *films, filmstrips, video cassettes, creative projects, dramatization, service projects.*

A two-pronged attack on the "blahs" should get you through the slump season: (1) recharge your own spirits and (2) change your pace with your students. Good luck!

17

How Can We Use Co-Teachers and Helpers?

"I love being a catechist, but I'm tempted to quit. I have to take attendance, set up projectors, hand out and pick up worksheets and supplies, help those with special learning needs, and be sure the room is in order as well as teach. With all these things to do, I don't see that I'm becoming a better catechist. I'm not growing."

Your experience is sadly too common. We've shared it ourselves. We recall how often we have felt that we would not sign up to teach again the next September.

But we have discovered a very practical way to grapple with the kind of situation you describe. Our solution is to divide up the work in one of two ways:

a) have a *co-catechist,* or
b) have a *catechist helper.*

Let's begin with the latter.

A Catechist Helper

We try whenever possible to have a catechist helper working with us. The catechist helper does all the things you mentioned as keeping you from being able to function fully as a catechist.

Some of the responsibilities of such a helper would include these:

• *Before Class Begins.* Before class the helper makes sure the door is unlocked, the room is warm or cool enough, and clean. He or she sees that the needed equipment, supplies, and materials are in their proper places, that the equipment is in working condition and properly set up, that textbooks and other resources are at hand.

52

This leaves us free during the precious moments before class. We can review our lesson plan. We can pray for God's guidance. We can be available to students, and their parents, as soon as they begin to arrive. The helper's work frees us to create a hospitable environment in which we and our students can get to know one another more personally.

Sometimes the informal moments before or after class allow the more hesitant students to approach us with personal questions they dare not ask before their peers.

• *During Class.* Once class is underway, the helper is responsible for running equipment, distributing supplies and other resources, and taking attendance. He or she may also be present to individual students, encouraging and helping them.

We are thereby freed to devote our energies almost totally to our students and to what they are expected to learn. We are not distracted and torn with a variety of activities not directly related to being a catechist. We can experience more fully the rewards of watching young people learn about their faith and grow in that faith. We can be relaxed enough to listen and learn from those we teach.

• *After Class.* Once class ends our helper takes care of restoring the place to its original condition. She or he puts away equipment and supplies, closes windows, turns in the attendance sheet, and does whatever else is necessary.

We are free then to chat with the students and with any parents that drop in. We can also make any "after-action" notes about how the lesson went, how to carry it over into the next lesson. We can take a moment to thank God for guiding us and our students.

• *Some observations.* We have found that the helpers not only help us, but they find the experience rewarding and challenging. It is not unusual for catechist helpers to move on to become catechists.

We try to share with our helpers the importance of what they do. Theirs is a significant role in the catechetical ministry. Not only do the helpers free us to be more completely engaged with the students and the catechetical process, but they share in that process as well. At times a helper will be closer to individual students than we, and more able to help them.

Co-Catechists

In addition to, or in place of a helper, we have found that having a co-catechist can be most rewarding. Two catechists can share the teaching in a variety of ways.

One way we have found useful is to alternate classes. One catechist teaches one week, while the other observes and assists where possible.

Then they change places the following week. They may prepare each class together or each may be responsible only for preparing the classes he or she teaches.

Another way is to divide up tasks. Each may be stronger in some teaching skill: lecturing or explaining, involving the students in creative activities, leading the class in prayer, using media, keeping order. The co-catechists divide up their work on the basis of their strengths. So the students have the best of each catechist.

> • *Observations.* We have learned that for co-catechists to work well together they need to have a degree of mutual trust. Jealousy or trying to outshine the other is destructive.
>
> We have found married couples—when they are able to work together happily—give an added witness to the students by co-teaching.
>
> Co-catechists can learn a great deal from one another. There can be mutual enrichment, honest criticism, a shared striving to improve and grow, and shared prayer.

To be a good catechist is a challenging but rewarding task. When it is shared in a freeing way with a catechist helper or a co-catechist it can be an even more satisfying and enriching experience.

18

How Can We Involve Parents?

"My classes seem to be going well. The children and I like the textbook. They seem to be learning. But a question keeps nagging me. What about their parents? How can I get them more involved in their children's religious education?"

That's a very important question, one we've given much thought to over the years. Common sense and the Church's clear teaching points to the parents as their children's primary religious educators. Yet there is often little effort to relate what happens in parish or school religious education classes with what occurs at home.

Two key ideas about parental involvement lie behind the practical approaches we suggest below:

1. *Shared responsibility.* Parents freely grant us catechists a share in their responsibility for the faith growth of their children. In the process parents may not abdicate their primary responsibility, nor may we catechists take it on ourselves. So, we believe parents have a right and responsibility to be actively involved in all dimensions of the catechetical program.

2. *Two-way communication.* Responsible parental involvment in parish or school catechetical programs involves communication to and from parents. It is not just enough to keep the parents informed of what you are doing in class. They need to be able to give input as well.

Ways To Involve Parents

Here are nine ways we have found to put those two ideas into practice. You may need to adapt them to your particular situation.

1. Meetings. It is important for you and your students' parents to have personal contact at times during the year.

One or two *formal* parent-catechist meetings a year may suffice to get acquainted and to discuss goals, content, textbook, schedule, and other aspects of the program. Special meetings may be needed with individual parents as the year goes on to discuss progress or problems. A celebration and evaluation can be an affirming way to end the year.

Even more helpful at times are occasional *informal* meetings as parents drop-off or pick-up children or just bump into you in church, supermarket or workplace. Such meetings can be invaluable sources of more personal knowledge of the parents and a feel for the family situation of a student.

At all of these meetings it is as important for you to *listen* to the parent's ideas and feelings as to *inform* them of your goals and plans. In this way they can become more responsible and involved.

2. Telephone. One or two calls to each family during the year assures the parent of your genuine interest and gives you a chance to invite criticisms and suggestions.

3. Notes/letters. One of the most appreciated things we do is write a brief *weekly letter* to the parents of our students. We share with them what we attempted to do that week, give them references to or summaries of any books or other media we used, and suggest one or two ways they might reinforce the classroom learning at home during the week. This takes a little time and effort, but parents each year single out the weekly letters as the most helpful thing we do for them.

4. Textbook. We see the religion textbook as a vital bridge between ourselves as catechists and our students' parents. Sometimes in CCD programs, catechists keep the textbooks in the classroom since children tend to forget to bring them in once-a-week settings. In such cases catechists need to find ways for parents to see the text books from time to time.

5. Student work. Parents are normally most interested in what their children do in religion class. *Homework* is one way of letting parents see and also take part in what their children are doing. Again, in once-a-week settings homework is often not realistic. Better than homework, perhaps, is what the children do or make in class. *Worksheets* or *projects* done in class need to be shared with the parents. Parents may be invited to collaborate in some projects.

6. Family Mass. Once a year we have a family Eucharist for our students and their parents. The students plan the liturgy and are actively involved in as many ways as possible. Enjoying appropriate refreshments after Mass allows for informal contact among parents and also with you, the catechist.

7. Guest teachers. At times one or more parents have particular knowledge, interest or skills directly related to a unit or lesson. Invite them to teach that class or to co-teach it with you.

8. Room parents. We invite parents to take responsibility for various support aspects of the program, e.g. supplying snacks, notifying other parents, accompanying field trips, and other tasks.

9. Observers. Be sure the parents feel free to come occasionally to observe your classes. Few will do so, but the invitation reveals your awareness of their rights and responsibilities.

We hope you find one or more of these ideas helpful. You are right on target with your concern about involving parents more actively.

19
What Resources Are Available?

"We are using what most of the teachers think is a good textbook, but I don't feel it is very creative. I want to find ways to go beyond the lesson plans in the textbook, but I'm not familiar with other resources. What would you recommend?"

We have often shared your feeling of wanting to "go beyond" or to "do more." Even the best of textbooks can seem somewhat lacking to a catechist who feels as you do.

So where can you turn for other resources?

Our view of resources for any teaching-learning situation—and especially for catechesis—reflects our educational convictions. We believe that learners are also teachers and teachers must be learners, too. We believe that both teachers and learners are much more creative than they believe. And we believe catechesis needs to remain close to ordinary life. So here are our resource recomendations.

Resource #1: Holy Spirit

We believe that the Holy Spirit is active throughout the whole teaching-learning process. Christ's Spirit is the most essential resource. It is the Spirit who opens the heart and mind to grasp the mystery of life in Christ. It is vital to pray for the Spirit's creative spark and to be as open as you can be to the movement of the Spirit throughout the entire teaching-learning process.

Resource #2: Students

We believe that our students are the next primary resource in the catechetical process. God's Word may he discerned in their experiences and in their creative works.

But for God's Word to be heard in the lives and creativity of your students you need to foster an atmosphere of mutual respect and trust. Otherwise there will be little honest self-sharing on their part. And, as a result, you and they will miss one of the most important catechetical resources. Creative activities by your students, expressing their knowledge, feelings and experience, tap into this vital resource. Such activities can be quite simple and inexpensive—like drawing, painting, writing, role-playing, dramatics, music, discussion and prayer.

Resource #3: Teacher/Catechist

Next to the Holy Spirit and your students you are the most important creative resource you have. Most of us tend to underestimate and underuse our abilities. It is to be expected that God speaks to you and your students through your experience, knowledge and feelings. Don't hide yourself from your students behind a wall of theological words unrelated to your life. Catechesis is an interpersonal sharing of faith more than an indoctrination of Church teachings and biblical facts.

So, reflect on your life, your faith, your studies. Draw upon your inner resources. Share something of yourself with your students. Coming to know you may be the most valuable catechetical experience your students will have. In you they may meet Christ Jesus.

Resource #4: Other People

Your parish and neighborhood, your family and acquaintances, include a variety of people who may be exciting resources for your catechesis. Some may be exceptional in some field, others may be moving examples of courageous ways to face difficulties, still others may have experiences or training related to a lesson you are teaching, and others may be compelling models of compassion, justice and peace. Many people would be honored to be invited to your class to share their gifts with your students.

Resource #5: Other Things

There are a world of things already in your home or school that are ready resources. Newspapers and magazines often have superb real life stories, great photos and art, delightful graphics, insightful cartoons and comics, puzzles, maps—many related to the same topics you are exploring in your textbook. The same is true of television programs.

You probably also have a wide assortment of all kinds of things that can be creative resources—paper, cardboard, string, yarn, plastic, wood, toys, paper cups, supermarket and trash bags, cloth, clothes hangers, photos, to name a few of the more obvious. Once you have a few rewarding experiences with such everyday resources, you will begin noticing even more readily available resources.

Resource #6: Published Works.

Books, films, filmstrips, records, slides, art masterpieces, audio- and video-cassettes, computer programs, games and other useful media are available from a variety of sources—libraries, galleries, book and music stores, toy stores, and catalogues. Your textbook probably lists carefully selected published resources.

These professionally prepared media can be very powerful when you use them skillfully and purposefully within your catechesis. But do not underestimate the power of resources more immediately at hand everyday, or that you and your students can create yourselves.

We hope our thoughts help you supplement your textbook in a more creative manner.

20

How Can We Make the Most of Summer?

"Classes end in two weeks. I must confess, I'm glad. It's been a good year, but I'm tired. I'm looking forward to summer vacation. I do want to teach again next year. Deep down I like being a catechist. Is there anything I can do during the summer to help me be a better catechist next fall."

Your question is a good one. We are looking forward to a change of pace during the summer, too. But being catechists is in our blood, as it is in yours, and we'll be teaching again next September.

Here are a few suggestions we and other catechists have found helpful for making the most of the summer break.

1. **Take Time to Debrief.** Even though you are eager to move away from your year-long teaching routine, you may find the summer months more fruitful if you take an hour to look back over the past year. Do your brief evaluation or debriefing alone, or with other catechists with whom you have been working. You might even involve your students in such a year-end-evaluation.

Keep it simple. What worked best? What did you and your students most enjoy and find most helpful? What didn't work? What are the areas in which you feel you need most improvement?

If you will be teaching another grade or using another textbook next year, take a look at the text to become sensitive to the major topics or themes you will be teaching and the general approach you will be expected to use.

Jot down the main points you want to be sure to remember and work on next fall.

Then put your notes and books away for the summer! Your subconscious will keep working quietly during vacation, helping you profit from your summer experiences in unsuspected ways that will enrich your teaching next year.

2. Enjoy the Summer. Perhaps the best preparation for next year's teaching is to enter fully into the opportunites the summer vacation presents. We tend to be so task oriented and busy during the school year that summer often allows time to "smell the flowers" and expand our imagination and sensitivities.

Play, beauty, relaxation, enjoyment of nature, being with family and friends, a more balanced schedule, travel—all these nurture a vital part of our lives.

Catechesis needs to flow out of ourselves more than out of text books, lesson plans, and media. The richer our experience, the more sensitive our spirits, the more in touch with ourselves, others, the created world and the Creator, the better our religious teaching may become.

3. Make a Retreat. Many catechists find a weekend or weeklong spiritual retreat of great value during the summer. This allows time to step back and look deeper into your life from a Christian faith perspective.

Retreat opportunities vary widely in location, methodology, cost and availability. Some are essentially individual, others are more group or family oriented. Check locally in your area, or consult sources like the summer listings of retreat opportunities that appear in the *National Catholic Reporter,* as well as ads or notices in diocesan newspapers and Catholic magazines.

If you cannot avail yourself of any of these opportunities, you might create your own mini-retreat.

Set aside a few moments each day for prayer and reflection. Use the Bible, a book or cassette to guide you. For example, Joan Chittister's two-book *Psalm Journal* (Sheed & Ward, Kansas City, MO 64141), would be a practical guide. So too would one of the many series of cassette retreats and spiritual conferences available from Credence Cassettes, (P.O. Box 419491 Kansas City, MO). Or read re-flectively during the summer a good book on spirituality or on a theological topic central to your coming year's teaching.

Your catechesis is ultimately the sharing of *your faith* as it becomes evident to your students in your life and words.

4. Participate in a Professional Workshop. More and more catechists find a weekend or week-long professional workshop on religious education, theology, Bible, liturgy, spirituality, psychology or education to be an exhilarating experience during the summer. Such a workshop can be fun, providing new insights and practical techniques. Workshops or seminars are available at many colleges and universities. Check with your diocesan religious education office, the national listings in the *NCR,* notices in magazines. We are on the faculty of the professional catechetical seminars offered in various cities by Silver Burdett & Ginn Publishing Company each summer (contact Religion Division, Silver Burdett & Ginn, 250 James Street, Morristown, NJ 07960 for information).

5. Learn Something New. Your catechesis will be richer—as will your personality and whole life—if you continue to grow and develop. Use the slower pace and increased leisure you may have during the summer to expand your knowledge and skills—in any area that interests you. It may be learning to dance, play the piano, cook, work with wood, create photographs, paint, repair cars, learn a language, fish, grow vegetables or roses—anything that expands your horizons and gives you satisfaction.

Best wishes for a relaxing, creative, renewing, fun summer!

21
Who, me? Creative?

"I wish I were a more creative teacher. Other catechists in our parish are always coming up with exciting classes. Mine seem dull and routine. I try hard but I just never come up with new ideas. What's wrong with me?"

There's probably nothing wrong with you. We have repeatedly asked catechists in workshops on creativity to name three creative people. Perhaps one in a hundred includes their own name on their list of three creative people.

Several years ago a major company, faced with a need to come up with new products, did a study of its employees to find those who were most creative. The results of the study are instructive: those who *thought* they were creative, were in fact doing creative work. They were creative because the *believed* they were creative.

Bill Moyers did a marvelous series of TV shows on creativity a few years ago. After interviewing people considered creative in various walks of life and studying the research on creativity, he came to two conclusions:

(1) *Everyone is creative;* and,

(2) *Creativity can be nurtured.*

After all, we are made in the image and likeness of the Creator!

What Is Creativity?

Creativity is *the ability to come up with something new out of your own unique individuality*—a new idea, a fresh insight, a new product, a novel way of doing something, a different way of teaching a lesson. Creativity typically results from *making connections* between what seems unrelated.

Almost all young children exhibit immense creativity. After childhood, sadly, people typically show less and less creativity.

Why Are We So Uncreative?

Why do most of us feel we are lacking in creativity. Experts point to certain factors that dampen or even extinguish our natural, God-given creativity. You may recognize some of these in your own experience.

• Fear of failure keeps us from trying something new;

• Criticism by others or by ourselves often makes us doubt ourselves, stifling our creativity;

• Rigid mental habits ("We always do it that way") tend to prohibit looking for new ways;

• Time pressure and stress, which at times spark creativity, often stifle it by keeping us feeling "boxed in," powerless;

• Reluctance to play, perhaps because of an excessive "work ethic," blocks the free association of ideas;

• Apathy or laziness prevents the work creativity presupposes.

What Makes Us More Creative?

We can nurture our own creativity by consciously working against the factors that stifle creativity. We can also take some concrete, positive steps to become more creative. Here are a few, with a special focus on becoming a more creative catechist.

Creativity normally follows a certain rhythm or pattern involving five steps or phases. We will exemplify that pattern in terms of planning a more creative lesson.

(1) *Preparation.* Creative ideas rarely spring out of nowhere. Becoming a more creative catechist and planning more creative lessons requires

on-going preparation by living more creatively and faithfully, and by continuing professional development through catechetical courses, reading, and experience.

(2) *Concentration.* After teaching one class, begin soon to plan the next class. Study the lesson plan. Note any questions or problems you have with it. Examine other resources. Do background reading.

If possible, do this *with one or more catechists* who may be planning the same lesson. *Brainstorm* ideas, that is, come up with *as many ideas for the class as possible.* Jot them down *without judging or criticizing* them. Only when you run dry go back over the whole list and *select* the most promising ideas.

This initial planning work *concentrates* and *focuses* your mind on the up-coming class, and turns on your creative juices. It brings your broad preparation to bear on an individual lesson plan.

(3) *Incubation.* Then go about your business until shortly before the next class. Your *unconscious* mind will continue to work and play with your lesson plan.

Attitudes and activities that nurture your creativity during this incubation period—as well as during the whole of your life, include:

• *Affirming your creativity,* by telling yourself you *are* creative, and by celebrating any creative thing you do, no matter how small.

• *Expanding your horizons* by reading more widely than you tend to, talking with interesting people, visiting museums, traveling. Let new images, new ideas into your mind. Learn to listen to your inner stimuli as well as outer ones.

• *Relaxing and playing more.* Make leisure time to enjoy yourself, whether it be going shopping, playing or watching sports, fishing, painting, walking—anything you really enjoy and find relaxing.

(4) *Illumination* is the fourth phase in the creative pattern. When you least expect it a new idea for your class may seemingly just pop into your head. To capture such ideas, it helps to *carry a notepad* with you to jot down any new ideas.

(5) *Production.* Finally the time comes to put it all together. Sometime prior to the class, sit down with your books, your new ideas, and carefully design your final, creative lesson plan.

Following this rhythm of *"work, relax and play, work,"* you may be surprised at how creative you are.

22

How Can We Ask Really Good Questions?

"I have the growing feeling that my classes rarely get below the surface. The youngsters learn facts, and especially Bible stories, well. But it all seems to stay on a superficial level. I wonder some times how much the stories and facts mean to them. At times it all seems so superficial. Any suggestions?"

Your experience is not unusual. In fact you are grappling with one of the most challenging tasks every catechist faces. Superficiality stifles catechesis and stultifies faith growth.

We have found in our own experience that one of the most effective ways to break through the surface and minimize superficial catechesis is *good questioning.*

The great theologian, Karl Rahner, believed that good questions are signs of God's alluring presence in our lives. Faith grows through questioning, probing, exploring.

Basic Attitudes

Good catechetical questioning flows from three *basic attitudes:*

#1: You, as catechist, as teacher, need to have an open, questioning mind, searching more deeply yourself into the mystery of life and Catholic faith.

#2: You need to respect your students' abilities and desires, believing that they are able and want to learn.

#3: You need to believe that you can learn from your students as well as teach them. You can learn *with* and *from* those you teach.

Kinds of Questions

Assuming that you are growing in those attitudes, you may find it helpful to look at *four kinds of catechetical questions*. These four kinds of questions relate to human experiences as well as to aspects of our Catholic faith tradition. We will exemplify each kind of question in terms of the "sacraments."

1. Fact Questions. These are obvious questions to ensure accurate knowledge of important facts. For example, "How many sacraments are there?," "What is a sacrament?" We want our students to learn basic Catholic teachings, rituals, prayers, historical facts. Fact questions are important, but may easily remain on a superficial level.

2. Meaning Questions. "What does that mean?" flows naturally from a statement of fact, a biblical story, or a doctrinal definition. That simple question may quickly reveal the different understandings your students have of the very same definition of "sacrament."

Meaning questions invite your students to go below the surface of their factual knowledge of life and faith.

3. Value Questions. It is important to move still deeper with more personal questions. Value questions bring the teaching closer to home, for example: "What difference does it make to you that there are sacraments?" "What place do the sacraments have in your life?" "How do you feel about the sacraments?"

Since these are much more personal questions, you need to ask them with respect for your students' privacy and sensitivity. Never force a student to answer value questions. Rather work to create an atmosphere of mutual trust where students feel free to express where they really are in terms of life experiences and Catholic teaching or practice.

4. Ultimate Questions. The deepest level of questioning in catechesis probes the most profound questions of life. Ultimate or limit questions touch down into life's mystery.

For example, following up on questions of fact, meaning, and value, you might ask about sacraments: "What do the sacraments suggest about life and death? about good and evil? about true happiness? about the world and the human heart? about God?"

Such questions touch on the depths of human experience and Catholic faith. They may not be glibly, neatly answered. They are answered best by silent wonder, trusting faith, and humble prayer. Story, symbol, silence, ritual are the privileged means of responding to life's ultimate questions. It is a great gift to your students to open them gradually to these questions— every answer to which brings with it a further question. For at its depth human experience opens to the inexplicable mystery of God.

How To Ask Questions

There are several helpful ways of asking all four kinds of questions to help engage students on a deeper level of thought and discussion.

#1. Rarely ask questions that can be answered with a simple "Yes" or "No."

#2. Normally ask a question of the whole class before directing it to any particular individual. This invites all to try to answer your question.

#3. Questions can be asked in a variety of creative ways, for example: by throwing a student's question back to the questioner or to the whole class, or by using poems, pictures, stories, popular songs, movies, and other media and creative activities.

#4. Simply refuse to accept superficial answers. Challenge the students to think more deeply.

Good questioning is one of the most important skills you need to work on if you want to break through the surface-learning you experience in your classes. Once your students feel free to ask *their real questions* you will know that your teaching has gotten below the surface.

23
What About Memorizing?

"When I grew up, I had to memorize countless catechism questions and answers. But when my children were in school, they never seemed to have anything to memorize in religion. Now I'm a catechist and wonder what to do about memorizing. Should I insist on a lot of memory work or not?"

Your question is shared by many catechists and parents. The pendulum swing you describe confuses many.

Our view is that both extremes—memorizing almost everything, and memorizing almost nothing—are defective. But there is a real place for *selective memorization* in catechesis.

The *National Catechetical Directory* for the United States recalls that "memorization has . . . had a special place in the handing-on of faith throughout the ages and should continue to have such a place today, especially in catechetical programs for the young" (#176,e).

Why Memorize?

Memorization is important in catechesis for several reasons.

1. Owning. Learning by heart what you have explored and studied often helps you make it more fully your own—owning it. The process of memorizing allows you to make what you learned a conscious part of who you are. It becomes part of your very identity, helping you remain aware of who you are as a Catholic. For example, the Our Father, prayed at home from an early age, can become part of one's lifelong identity as a follower of Jesus.

2. Banking. While memorizing is primarily valuable for making your own what you are presently learning, it also can be useful for future situations. Memorized formulations of Christian wisdom or prayer can become a lifelong resource to be tapped into as needed.

For example, Psalm verses learned by heart years earlier may rise up as genuine prayer in moments of joy or sorrow, success or failure.

3. Bonding. Memorizing basic formulations of Catholic faith can provide a powerful feeling of unity with others who share that same faith tradition. Even small children can feel more fully part of the parish community as all pray together the Our Father at Sunday Mass. Knowing by heart basic Catholic faith formulations can also foster bonding or connectedness with those of past and future generations who share that same Catholic tradition.

These are some of the key catechetical reasons for memorization. There are also pedagogical values in memorizing that apply in catechesis as well as in other curriculum areas.

What To Memorize

What to memorize needs to be pondered carefully. Today's better religious education textbooks helpfully indicate what to have students memorize. The texts follow the guidance of the *NCD*, which suggests that basic formulas and factual information in the following areas deserve to be memorized by young and old:

1. *Basic prayers,* like the Sign of the Cross, Our Father, Hail Mary;

2. *Bible basics,* like key themes and persons, as well as major texts about God's love and care;

3. *Liturgical basics,* like the parts of the Mass, the sacraments, the Church seasons and major feasts;

4. *Doctrinal basics,* like the Apostle's Creed; and

5. *Moral and spiritual basics,* like the commandments, beatitudes, gifts of the Holy Spirit, works of mercy.

The *NCD* spells out the specifics more fully in #60; 143; 176e; 178.

How To Memorize

Individuals differ in how they best learn by heart, and teachers have their own special ways of helping students do memory work. So it may be helpful to reflect on your own experience. We would like to share a few tips we have learned.

1. Memorize only what has meaning. Rote memory of formulas the students do not understand has little value in catechesis. Normally memorization comes toward the end of the process, learning by heart what has been grappled with and understood.

2. Break it down. Don't have students memorize long texts all at once. Help them break longer texts like the Creed into smaller segments, for example, the parts of the Creed dealing with Father, Son, Spirit, Church, after life.

3. Make it fun. Memorization need not be boring nor burdensome. Use approaches like games, prizes, music, teamwork, worksheets, choral reading, to make the memorizing more enjoyable, and thereby more effective.

4. Repeat creatively. Since memorization tends to be gradual, repitition is most helpful. But too often repetition can be monotonously stifling. It needs to be creative. For example, worksheets of a longer text with missing words to be filled in can be repeated until all can fill in all the blanks. Each time different words may be missing.

We hope these brief thoughts on *Why, What,* and *How* to memorize are helpful to you in finding a balance between too much and too little memorization.

24

How Can We Help Children Learn To Pray?

"I always begin and end my classes with a prayer. But those I teach don't take it very seriously. I don't know what else to do, because I never was taught much about prayer. I'd be glad for any help you could give me."

For years we did just what you are doing, beginning and ending class with a prayer. Like you we gradually sensed that not much real prayer was going on.

We also learned, first from Fr. Gerard Sloyan at Catholic University, and later from the *National Catechetical Directory,* that "all catechesis is [to be] oriented to prayer and worship" (145). So we worked at finding better ways of helping our students learn to pray.

Here are some we found worked.

1. Pray Yourself. Probably the most important tip is to become a more prayerful person. The place to begin is to learn more about praying so you can pray more throughout your life. Try out in your own life the ways of learning to pray we describe here.

2. Foster Dispositions for Prayer. In prayer we express our trust in God, our gratitude to God, our awe at God's greatness and goodness, our sorrow for hurting our relationship with God, our petitions for God's help. If prayer is to be authentic, it must flow out of genuine wonder and appreciation, thanksgiving, honesty, repentance, trust, and affection.

We can expose our students to the marvels of creation, giving them opportunities to wonder. We can trust them, so they can learn to trust. We can express gratitude to them and guide them in learning to be thankful. We can apologize for hurting them, and forgive them for hurting us. In these ways we nurture the predispositions for prayer.

75

3. Plan for Meaningful Prayer. Prayer in class needs to flow out of what is happening in that class. Any praying should rise up out of the life experience being explored and be enriched by the Catholic prayer traditions reflected in the lesson. The praying should be done at one or two moments in the lesson where prayer best fits.

This requires careful planning. Your textbook undoubtedly provides guidance in its lesson plans. Experience will gradually give you a keener sense of which moments in a given lesson are best for prayer.

4. Expand Their Experience of Prayer. The traditions of Catholic spirituality provide a wealth of ways to pray. Fortunately, contemporary textbooks build various prayer forms into their lessons.

Here are just a few forms of prayer we find useful in classes.

• *Traditional Catholic prayers.* All Catholics should have a chance to learn common Catholic prayers and their meaning. The *National Catechetical Directory* mentions the Sign of the Cross, Lord's Prayer, Hail Mary, Apostles' Creed, Glory be to the Father, Acts of Faith, Hope and Charity, Act of Contrition, and Meal Prayers (143, 145, 176e). We have these and other prayers like St. Francis Peace Prayer, the Jesus Prayer and the Rosary, among others in our book, *Living Water: Prayers of our Heritage* (Paulist Press, 1978).

Vary how the students pray these prayers, for example: pray each word silently with every breath, allowing time to savor each word; or reflect on each word as long as the reflection is rewarding.

Try this latter way also by writing reflections on each word, or putting a drawing or photo with each word.

• *Biblical and liturgical prayers.* The Bible and liturgy are filled with prayers you may draw upon in your catechesis as well as in your own prayer life. The *Psalms* are perhaps the most loved prayers in both the Bible and the Liturgy. Use them often—whole Psalms, or just one or several verses, as they fit the themes of your lessons.

• *Meditation.* Meditation is a form of quiet reflection on daily experience, a Bible story or saying, a liturgical symbol or ritual, a doctrinal teaching, or a saint's life. It is a "mulling over," "pondering," in mind and heart. There are various methods of meditation. The *imagination* can be very helpful. Try to "see" what is happening, "hear" any spoken words, "feel" with any people involved.

Use *media* to facilitate meditation—a striking *photo* or an *art masterpiece, drawing* or *writing* one's thoughts and feelings, *music* played quietly in the background, or a *song* or *hymn* in which music and words together support meditation. *Physical position* may also facilitate reflection—sitting relaxed but erect, walking, kneeling.

• *Affective prayer.* Meditation often leads to praising God, expressing thanks, trust or love. We, and our students, may pray these "affective" prayers *silently* or *aloud,* in *writing* or *singing,* with *gesture* or other *art forms.*

• *Mantras.* A help to prayer in class or anytime is the slow, silent repetition of a *single word like "Jesus,"* or a *short phrase* like "My Lord and my God." Try repeating the "mantra" slowly with each breath.

• *Litanies.* Official litanies like the "Litany of the Saints" are occasionally suitable. Students can make up their own litanies in relation to what they learn in a lesson.

• *Spontaneous prayers.* At a suitable moment in a lesson, invite those who wish to do so, to pray aloud in their own words.

These are just some of the many possibliities for helping yourself and your students to pray more meaningfully. For further suggestions see *And The Children Pray,* by Janaan Manternach with Carl J. Pfeifer (Ave Maria Press, 1989).

25

How Can We Use Pictures?

"I recently read a surprising article in a business magazine. The writer urged executives and managers to use more visuals in meetings because most of what people learn today is learned through what they see. If that's true, I need to use more visuals in my religion classes, but I'm not sure how."

Some studies suggest that as much as 83% of what we learn comes to us through our eyes. As Confucius said centuries ago: "A picture is worth a thousand words."

Photos and art, especially religious art, are particularly important in catechesis. All through the Church's history catechists have used pictures—in catacombs, cathedrals, and catechisms. Photos and art are like windows into life's mystery and the Church's faith tradition.

There are countless ways to use photos and art effectively in catechesis. We have space here only to suggest several basic principles and some proven techniques.

1. Using Pictures: Basic Principles.

• *Select carefully.* Use really good photos and art, works that have the power to engage the viewer, evoke feelings, and invite deeper reflection on life and faith.

Look through magazines for strong, evocative photos and art. Notice ads. Look through art books and museums for good religious art.

Begin early to collect strong photos and art related to the themes and topics you will be teaching.

• *Study the visual before using it.* Look carefully at the picture, letting it speak to you. Notice your reactions. Examine details. Think of questions it suggests. Imagine ways of using it.

• *Move from global response to detailed analysis.* Allow the students to look quietly at the picture for a moment or two. Then invite them to share verbally or through some creative expression their *overall reaction* to the picture. For example, "What feelings does it arouse in you?" "What does it say to you?" "What is happening in the picture?"

Next guide them to *notice details* and their significance, for example, colors, lines, perspective, individual persons or objects.

• *Move from picture to persons.* Begin with the picture and the students' reaction to it. That is usually comfortable, non-threatening. Gradually guide the students to look at their own lives through the prism of the picture. Respectful of your students' feelings and rights to privacy, ask, for example, "When have you ever felt like that?" "Acted like that?" "Write a story of a time you were in a situation like that?" "What does the picture suggest about the attitudes and values of people your age?"

• *Move from individual responses to group sharing.* A single photo or work of art has the power to suggest a wide range of feelings and ideas in your students. Sharing these can enrich all, surface legitimate differences, invite respect for others' opinions and foster a sense of community. The sharing will often be more honest if the initial reflection on the picture was done privately in writing.

• *Move from picture study to prayer and action.* The reflection and sharing about the picture will lead hopefully to some deeper awareness of God's Word in daily life or in our Catholic faith tradition. The response to God's Word involves *prayer* and *action.* Photos and art can be marvellous helps to prayer of various kinds, especially meditation. They can also motivate you and your students to decide on actions suggested by what you discovered about life and faith through the picture.

2. Using Pictures: Helpful methods.

Here are some specific techniques of using pictures in catechesis:

• *Display.* Hang a photo or art work to draw attention to the theme of your lesson or unit. It may arouse curiosity, foster interest, and be a visual focal point to which you can return from time to time.

• *Caption/title.* Invite your students to write captions or titles that say in words what the picture says to them nonverbally. Or, ask them to find a Bible verse that would be a suitable caption. Or, give them a Gospel verse as a caption and invite them to find a photo that it would fit.

• *Searching.* Give the students magazines. Have them find visuals that speak to them about the theme of your lesson, e.g. "trust."

• *Juxtapose.* Invite the students to place side by side two visuals they feel are similar in meaning or are opposites. Or have them juxtapose a piece of religious art, e.g. a Gospel story, with a photo they feel relates to it.

• *Tell story.* Show a photo or work of art. Ask the students to tell—verbally, in writing, or by acting—a story the visual suggests.

• *Collage.* Ask the students to cut out photos and art and paste them to posterboard to express a particular theme or message.

• *Create photo essay or slide show.* Give the students a large selection of photos or slides. If photos, invite them to create a story or essay with the photos, adding some commentary with words. If slides, have them create a slide show, with or without voice and music.

• *Give gifts.* At Christmas and other feasts, give your students small religious art reproductions, available from art museums and religious goods stores.

There are many more ways to use visuals in catechesis. We hope these few suggestions help you start.

26
How Can We Use Writing?

"My religion textbook seems to go overboard with writing. Some of it seems like busy-work, filling in blanks, completing sentences. When more challenging writing is called for, I spend most of the time spelling words for the kids. What does this have to do with religion?"

As authors of religion text books we feel a bit defensive at the moment. But we have not the slightest doubt about the value of writing in religious education. Nor are we unaware of the limited writing skills of many youngsters.

Why Write in Catechesis?

We use writing all the time in our religion classes. In our experience, few activities have been as revealing and rewarding as writing.

Why? We feel that writing gives people—children, youth, adults—*a special means of getting in touch with the mystery of who they are* and *what the world is like.*

Purposeful, creative writing allows individuals to "dialogue with themselves and with the world in which they live," as Elizabeth-Anne Vanek puts it. This kind of *reflective inner dialogue* is at the heart of faith growth.

The more creative writing activities in catechesis are meant to help students dig into their *experience* and their *Catholic tradition* and develop tools for expressing the mysteries encoded in both.

Some Principles of Writing for Faith-Growth

We have several principles for facilitating faith growth through creative writing.

81

• *Catechesis is not a writing class.* Our interest is in the expression of *meaning* and *feelings* in what the students write. We do help a bit with spelling, but our task is not to teach grammar, punctuation, spelling and similar skills.

• *Almost every student can write.* Except for those who have writing-related disabilities, we believe anyone can be helped *to write whatever they can say.* Many people fear writing because it seems hard and governed by so many rules. We work to free students from such fears, assuring them they *can* write what they think and how they feel, and encouraging *free, creative, imaginative* writing that flows out of their hearts and minds.

• *Have them write before and after talking.* Writing about an experience or belief *before* the class begins discussing and learning about it ensures more honest reflection by each individual and gives everyone an equal chance to share their insights. Otherwise the more vocal and assertive dominate discussions. *After* the group learning, writing allows individuals to assimilate and personalize what they have learned.

• *Have them fill the page.* We normally expect our students to fill the page rather than just write a sentence or two and give up. Most people have far more to say about almost anything than they and their teachers believe. There are, of course, some writing tasks that require only a few words.

What and How To Write

There is no limit to what to write about in catechesis, nor how or in what form to write. Here are some practical tips.

• *Writing stories* about experiences and beliefs tends to reveal and express much more than abstract definitions. We often ask students to write "real" or "pretend" stories to encourage greater honesty. Sometimes we ask them to write a story about a situation in a photo.

Stories may be very simple like "a time I learned to trust," a Bible story, a modernized version of a Bible story, or more complex, like a cartoon story, a film or TV script, a photo-essay.

• *Writing poems* may be an even more effective way of probing and expressing experiences and beliefs. We encourage free-form poems, but at times use fixed forms like haiku, cinquain, or diamonte to provide a ready-made structure.

• *Writing prayers* allows students to pray in their own words.

• *Writing definitions* can reveal deeper insights or misunderstandings. We often ask students to write what they mean by, say, "grace," "sin," "Church," "prayer," or "happiness," "friendship," "freedom," "love"—depending on the lesson theme.

• *Writing captions* for a photo or painting often sparks new insights, reveals unsuspected feelings, raises issues, and fosters dialogue.

• *Writing descriptions* of, for example, "the inside of your parish church," or "how to celebrate the Sacrament of Reconciliation," encourages accurate observation and may give rise to wonder and questions about the place or rite.

• *Writing bumper stickers and ads* is a fun way of probing and expressing beliefs and convictions.

• *Writing "translations"* of theological language—like "grace," "salvation"—into readily understandable words may raise meaningful questions and ensure understanding.

• *Writing letters or notes* can build a sense of ownership of what is learned and a desire to share it. It is also a way of reaching out with thanks and love to others and to work for justice and peace.

• *Writing "newspapers"* engages students in almost every form of creative writing.

• *Writing journals* enables more habitual, sustained reflection and provides a record of growth.

• *Writing reactions to news reports or stories,* often with worksheets we prepare, tends to bring out students' real faith convictions in relation to real life.

Those are but some of the many ways creative writing can encourage growth in faith.

27

How Can We Use Story and Poetry?

"Last year a friend gave me a book called The Read Aloud Handbook. *My wife and I have started reading stories to our children. They really enjoy it. What I'm wondering is whether reading stories like that might also work in teaching religion."*

We are delighted that you've discovered the joy of reading stories to your children at home. Be sure to thank your friend for giving you Jim Trelease's great book. It is one of our favorites.

We want to encourage you to follow up your idea about reading stories in your religion classes. We read a short piece of children's literature in every religion class for primary and intermediate aged children, and often with older youngsters and adults.

We also use a lot of poetry with all ages, including adults.

We are really just following *Jesus' example*. He did almost all of his teaching by telling stories and using poetic language.

Why Stories and Poetry in Catechesis?

In addition to Jesus' example, we use stories and poems for several reasons:

• *People like stories.* One obvious reason is the one you discovered with your own children—people like stories and poetry.

• *Stories break life open.* Stories are like a slice of life held up for appreciation and understanding. From them we and those we teach discover more of what life is really like.

• *Stories help us learn who we are.* Stories help people clarify their identity. A good story or poem puts us in touch with our own experiences through the story's characters. By identifying with them as they enjoy life's good things or struggle with life's many challenges, we probe in a pleasurable way who we are.

• *Stories inspire and motivate.* Watching story-people win out over evil, act courageously, honestly, compassionately and justly, provides an inner motivation to do in our lives what the attractive, admirable story characters do in theirs. We may also find reasons to hope.

For deeper insight into the value of story in catechesis, see Madeleine L'Engle, *Trailing Clouds of Glory—Spiritual Values in Children's Books* (Westminster, 1985).

Some Helpful Principles for Using Stories and Poems in Catechesis

With a willingness to experiment, you will find a variety of ways to use stories in your lessons.

Here are four important *principles* to keep in mind:

• *Plan carefully.* A story or poem must honestly fit the theme and goals of a particular lesson, and fit into the movement and rhythm of the class development.

• *Select carefully.* You need to *read beforehand* any book or poem you intend to use in class. If you don't enjoy it and find it insightful, chances are good your students won't either.

There are a number of helpful guides to good children's literature, in addition to Jim Trelease's *Read Along Handbook* (Penguin Books, 1985) which you have. We've liked Joanne Oppenheim, Barbara Brenner, and Betty D. Boegehold *Choosing Books for Kids* (Ballentine Books, 1986), and Eden Ross Lipson *The New York Times Parent's Guide to the Best Books for Children* (Times Books, 1988).

Other catechists and your local librarian may be very helpful in pointing out good stories and poems. Another rich source of good stories is the *reading curriculum* used in local schools.

• *Don't moralize.* Let the story or poem stand on its own. Don't tell the students its "point" or "moral." Rather, let them tell you what the poem or story says to them about life, about themselves.

Some Practical Tips for Using Story and Poetry in Catechesis

Here are some tested ways of using good stories and poems in your religion classes.

• *Read the story aloud.* The first is just what you do at home with your children. Read the story out loud to them. Try holding the book upside down, facing your class, and read it upside down so your listeners can also enjoy the illustrations. A little practice will make this easy.

• *Tell the story.* Some stories are better told than read. Telling a story or reciting a poem from memory can be a more personal experience since there is no book between you and your hearers. Practice a story until you feel comfortable telling it.

• *Let students read.* We often invite those we teach to read aloud stories and poems in their text books. Sometimes we ask one to read the whole story or poem; sometimes we let several read sections of the story in order. At other times we have them all read in silence.

• *Show a film, filmstrip, or video version of a story or poem.* Superb media presentations of great stories and poems are available. Ask your librarian or media expert.

• *Dramatize a story.* Occasionally your students might dramatize a story. We've done this both in class and during the Sunday Eucharist.

• *Visualize a story.* It can be fascinating to have your students visualze a story you've read or told, Try it with drawings or paintings, photos or slides.

• *Leave story open-ended.* Stop reading or telling a story shortly before the end. Invite your students to come up with how they think the story ends. Afterwards read them the actual ending.

Good luck as you bring the world of story and poetry into your catechesis.

28
How Can We Use Music and Song?

"Religion textbooks urge me to use music in my lessons. It sounds like a great idea, except for people like me who have tin ears and can't sing a note. Then, too, the kids seem only to turn on to rock, which I can't stand, and which isn't exactly religious anyway. So, what do you suggest?"

Your letter strikes a chord in our hearts. As religion textbook authors we often urge catechists to use music, songs, and hymns. As catechists we share many of your hesitations. Perhaps some tips we've learned may be helpful to you.

Music and Catechesis

We often remind ourselves of how important music and song have been for catechists down through the centuries. Some of the oldest parts of the New Testament are early Christian catechetical hymns (e.g. Philippians 2:5-11). Effective catechists and missionaries ever since have instinctively valued the unique power of music.

Music can touch a person's whole being—body, feelings, mind, heart. Music and song bring out the rich meaning of a message by echoing its inner feelings. Modern advertisers rely strongly on music's motivational power. Music moves us.

Music, especially rock, has become the common language of the young, almost the atmosphere in which they live. We feel, based on our recent classroom experience, that its use in catechsis is vital.

Using Music and Song

Here are some practical uses of music in your religion classes:

1. *To set a mood*, play music that supports the feelings of the message of your lesson: peaceful, happy, sad, meditative, angry. Play good music, for example, while the students arrive or work quietly.

2. *To explore meaning*, use a popular song that deals with the life theme, issue, or basic question of your lesson. Many contemporary songs, including rock, do this in a way your youngsters may readily relate to. Let them listen to the song. Then guide them in reflecting on and discussing the song's lyrics in relation to their lives.

3. *To tell a story*, select a Gospel song, an ancient ballad, or contemporary country hit, that fits your lesson. We have a rich American heritage of Gospel music to draw upon. The music adds feeling and interest to the story, also making it easier to remember.

4. *To teach a message*, find or make up (with the students) a song that summarizes a lesson's message. St. Francis of Asissi did this as a missionary catechist in India. St. Robert Bellarmine took popular love songs and changed their lyrics to convey his catechetical message. Writing new lyrics to songs your students know can be a creative way of helping them own a lesson's message. Many "secular" songs, including rock, already sing of basic beliefs and values.

5. *To pray*, use hymns that express the idea and sentiments of a lesson. Where possible, use hymns that the students also sing in their parish, to help them link their catechesis with Sunday liturgy. Or have the students write prayerful lyrics to a song melody they like.

But I Still Need Help!

Most of us need help in using music in our classes. We may not feel able to sing or lead singing. We may not know many songs to choose from for our classes. Luckily help is at hand. A few examples.

1. *Use a cassette or record player*. Equipment for playing music and songs is widely available and easy to use. Most schools, parishes, families, or even your students have such equipment. With songs, invite the students

to sing along, or work with its lyrics as they listen. Simply play mood music.

2. *Use helpers.* Draw upon the talents of your students and/or others who are more musically gifted. Many young people today play musical instruments. Look also to other teachers, parents or relatives of students, parishioners, friends, or neighbors. People often feel honored to be asked to use their talents for the good of others.

3. *Use other resources.* Here are some resources we have found useful.

We found our *students* to be experts at finding currently popular songs to use in class.

Be sure to look through your *religion textbook* for lists of recommended music or songs. Look also at your students' *music textbooks* for songs you can use.

Some *Catholic newspapers and magazines* have regular features on popular music and hit songs. An invaluable resource for appreciating and using rock music in religion classes is Father Don Kimball's *Top Music Countdown* (Tabor Publishing, P.O. Box 7000, Allen, TX 75002). Each issue selects 25 current rock hits and suggests ways of using them. Other features relate scripture themes to popular music, examine negative messages in current songs, have hints for parents, and describe successful uses of music in catechesis and liturgy.

We strongly encourage you slowly to make music and song a regular part of your catechesis. Take one step at a time to build up your confidence. Good luck!

29
How Can We Use Drawing and Painting?

"One of the things my students seem to enjoy is drawing. They can spend half a class drawing a picture. I really question how valuable drawing is in religion class, but the textbook keeps suggesting it. What do you think?"

We've observed that children, youth, and even adults seem to take to drawing more now than in years past. It may be because our culture has become so visually oriented.

We've also become more convinced from our experience that drawing and painting have great value in catechesis. For some, who are visual learners, drawing or painting is particularly important.

Why Draw or Paint?

Drawing and painting allow young or old to tap into and express their experience, insights, and feelings—in a pleasurable way.

Drawing involves *reflection*. Through line, shape and color people can often come to understand and express more about what they really believe than they are able to express in words. Drawings are like windows into an individual's spirit.

Completed drawings or paintings are great means of freeing people to share their thoughts and feelings—to *dialogue*. Talking about each other's drawings not only enriches individuals' insights but builds a sense of community.

Finished drawings may also be used for *prayer*, just as one might use an icon or art masteriece to encourage prayer. They can also be used to stimulate *action*, much as a strong photo, poster or ad calls out for actions like helping the hungry.

In these ways drawing and painting become powerful media for faith growth (see Chapter 4).

Using Drawing in Catechesis

Over the years we have learned some practical helps we are happy to share with you.

• *Technique is secondary.* Drawing or painting in catechesis is somewhat different than in an art class. Our main concern is not with artistic technique, but with the *meanings* and *feelings* that are expressed.

• *Encourage free expression.* Unfortunately many youngsters and adults have been drilled to "stay within the lines" when coloring, or to depict people and things only in realistic forms and colors ("grass can't be purple, it must be green").

Often, too, children draw small, cramped, pictures, using only a tiny portion of a large paper. Many also feel a need to draw first in pencil and then color over and within the lines.

We work to free them from these constrictions, urging more spontaneous, large, colorful, imaginative drawings or paintings.

• *Foster cooperation.* Drawing can at times be a great activity to do together. We sometimes have students work in pairs to create a drawing or painting. At other times we invite larger groups or the whole class to make a mural on the chalk board or long sheets of paper. We've also had groups create a slide show with drawings done on "write-on" slides (available at camera stores).

• *Affirm the students* in their efforts to express themselves. Honest words of praise, focusing on genuinely fine aspects of their work, help release their unique powers of expression.

• *Display and use.* Displaying the students' work is a way of affirming them all and enabling them to share and appreciate each other's insights. We try to use some of the students' drawings or paintings in subsequent sessions where they fit the themes of the lessons.

What To Draw in Catechesis

There is practically no limit as to what students may fruitfully draw or paint in catechesis. Here are a few kinds of things we often ask our students to draw.

• *An experience.* Drawing personal experiences is a rich way of helping those we teach (as well as ourselves) to see into what is happening in their lives. For example, asked to draw "your world," our 3rd graders a few years ago, drew pictures showing a world totally devoid of interaction with caring adults.

To add a note of humor, at times we suggest they draw the experience in the form of a comic strip or cartoon.

• *A Bible story.* Drawing or painting biblical stories can bring fresh insight into the stories. One of our recent 7th-grade student's drawing of Pentecost revealed some of the disciples huddled in fear of the Spirit coming into their lives. We had never thought of that before.

• *A liturgical symbol or ritual.* We recently asked our 4th graders to draw a picture of what the Eucharist means to them. Their drawings were revealing—a Bible, a chalice and host, a crucifix, a dove (Holy Spirit), a church, a burning candle, a world globe. Together, their pictures provided a rich summary of what the Eucharist really is.

• *A feeling or conviction.* We often ask our students to draw how it feels, for example, to be lonely, to be loved, to be rejected. A 2nd-grader's drawing of a small boy surrounded by a whole page of dark grey haunts us after more than a decade. Sometimes we challenge them to draw a feeling using only line and color, without people or recognizable objects.

• *A challenge.* We've found the drawing of ads a fascinating way for students to deepen and express a conviction, like "happiness comes more from giving than getting," or "Christians are called to make peace."

We hope our observations spark in you a renewed interest in using drawing and painting in catechesis.

30

How Can We Use Gesture and Movement?

"The youngsters I teach have so much energy. They seem to find it hard to sit still. Some are more active than others, including one who is obviously hyperactive. I'm at a loss as to how to channel their energies. They get so restless. Do you have any secret methods?"

We experience this with children and youth of all age levels, especially in once-a-week classes that meet after school or on school day evenings. We have no magic formula. Here are some tips learned over the years.

Appreciate Physical Energy

Our first suggestion is to try to make the most of students' energy rather than view it too negatively.

If the students, for whatever reason, seem to need more activity, we find ways to make our classes more active. Our bodies are vital for learning, communication, and action.

Some students learn primarily through bodily movement. Their learning style is called "haptic" or "kinesthetic," because they learn best when their bodies are actively engaged, moving, doing.

Involve the Whole Person

There are many ways to introduce more bodily movement into your classes without chaos resulting. But doing so takes careful planning, taking into account your level of tolerance for physical activity during class, the kind of space in which you teach, and what you are teaching. Some possibilities:

• **Move around during class.** A first step might be to build into each class several moves from place to place in the room where you teach. For example, read and write in one place or "learning center." Pray in another.

Do creative activities in still another. We often introduce a moment of exercise as part of the movement from one learning center to another.

• **Move outside your room.** Sometimes we have found it helpful to extend the movement to space outside the room for part of a class. For example, weather permitting, go outside, or go to another room for an activity, to a chapel or prayer room for prayer.

• **Have more active activities.** Another help is to introduce activities that involve greater physical involvement. Here are a few:

• *Play games.* A fun way to involve physical movement and gesture is to play a game like charades. Each student attempts to convey through body-language alone a certain experience, story, ritual or truth, as all try to guess what is being said without words.

There also are many active "simulation games" which play out common situations or complex social, economic or political issues.

• *Role-playing.* One way to help students explore their experiences through physical movement is role-playing. Individuals or small groups act out a significant experience in their lives, or in other people's lives. We've had small children, for example, act out a drooping flower's reaction to water or sun. One memorable class had older youngsters role-playing "being tempted to steal something."

Role-playing works particularly well for exploring interpersonal conflicts, like jealousy between peers, or arguments with parents. Social justice issues also lend themselves to role-playing, for example, "as you walk down the street a beggar approaches you."

• *Dramatics.* Dramatizing a Bible story, a liturgical rite, a saint's life or a piece of children's literature is another meaningful way to add physical activity to a class. You may present the students with a script or let them work one out themselves. Depending on the story and the time allotted, they might arrange a "set," prepare "props," and make "costumes."

• *Do hands-on activities.* There is a whole world of arts-and-crafts kinds of creative activities from which you can draw. Your active students can make things that may help them get into the message of your lesson. Just a few examples from an almost unending list: banners, "stained-glass" windows, painted rocks, bookmarks, collages, clay figures, bread, wall plaques.

• *Do body sculptures.* Invite the students to create a "sculpture" using their combined bodies as the material. For example, a sculpture showing what "Church" really is. One student begins by taking an expressive position revealing his or her view of Church. Another builds on the first, reinforcing or modifying the meaning, and so on until all are united in a physical statement of what "Church" means to them.

• *Pray with gestures.* Prayers prayed with gestures can have added meaning. We often pray the Lord's Prayer with gestures. Any prayer or hymn can be enriched with gestures. You and your students can work out appropriate gestures and movement.

• *Have processions.* An occasional procession can be meaningful and engage active youngsters. For example, process with the Bible from the room entrance, around the room, to enthrone the Bible in its place.

• *Dance.* Used occasionally and for special events, dance can be a very meaningful involvement of bodily movement and gesture in catechesis. Help the students work out simple dance movments to a song or hymn.

These are some ways we have found to help our students learn through bodily gesture and movement. We hope you try one or two.

31
How Can We Do Service Projects?

"I feel terrible. What I thought would be a great project turned out to be a disaster. I took my sixth graders to visit a nursing home. Many of the children were very upset by the experience. Some of the elderly patients were hurt when children pulled back from them. It was a very negative experience for us all. What went wrong?"

We've had similar experiences and understand your dismay. We will share what we learned from our mistakes. Perhaps you will find some of our suggestions helpful.

The Value of Service Projects

Despite discouraging negative experiences, it is important not to give up on worthwhile projects such as you describe. The Church today is convinced that "service" is one of the four major tasks of catechesis (see Chapter 1). So-called "service projects" are not an option or extra. They are part of our catechetical efforts to guide our students into a Christlike way of living. Compassion and justice are close to the heart of Jesus' lifestyle. It is vital that our children be involved in experiences that place them in contact with people who are in need and hurting.

Practical Guidelines

Here are some suggestions drawn from our experience and that of others. Successful service projects require careful planning, sensitive execution, and thoughtful follow-up.

Before: Careful Planning

It is imperative that you and your students plan carefully any service project, but especially those which involve sensitive interaction with persons with whom your children have had little previous contact.

Motivation. Take time together to reflect on the proposed project in the light of the Gospel and in relation to the content of your textbook that year. The children need to see the project as flowing from what they believe as Catholic Christians.

Arrangements. Work carefully beforehand with the responsible persons at the institution you plan to work with, for example: nursing home, soup kitchen, social agency, justice-peace office, orphan home, housing project. Learn any regulations they have; listen to their suggestions; ask about potential problems. Where possible, involve older students in working out these arrangements.

Raising Awareness. Take sufficient time to explore sensitively the upcoming project with the students. Make clear any rules, regulations or expectations the agency involved has set down. Explore with them any feelings and questions they may have about the coming experience. Prepare them for perhaps unexpected reactions, e.g. that lonely elderly persons may want to touch or hold them, or may be impassive, that poor persons may not express gratitude for their services.

At the same time help them realize what they may learn and receive from the very people they are helping. Those in need often have as much to share with us who serve them as we have to offer them.

Praying together. Pray that Jesus' Spirit be with them so that their project may actually benefit those they try to help, and also help them grow in Christ's way of living.

During: Sensitive Execution

Once the students are engaged in the actual project, you need to be present as a *participant observer*. Let the students do the work, but be sensitive to what they do and especially to how they are reacting. A social service professional or a trained staff member of the institution you are working with should also be on hand to assist.

Your involvement during the actual helping experience is primarily that of *support, encouragement, affirmation,* and *guidance,* where appropriate or needed.

After: Thoughtful Follow-up

Often neglected, but of extreme importance, is an opportunity for the youngsters to reflect with you on the experience. It is vital that they have a chance to share their perceptions and feelings, as well as any questions that the project raised for them.

Find time soon after the service experience for a relaxed follow-up or de-briefing. Here are a few of the areas you may want to reflect on together:

- What are your overall reactions to the experience?
- What did you learn from doing the project?
- What feelings did you have as you were with those you came to serve?
- How do you feel you helped them? How did they help you?
- What would you do differently if you were to do this project again?
- What questions did the project raise for you?
- How does what you did reflect the life and teachings of Jesus and the Church?

Share your own insights, feelings and questions with the students as they are sharing with you. Be sure they connect their service project with the Gospel message and the Church's teaching.

End with prayer, thanking God for helping them through this project, and asking God's continued blessing on those they served.

Summary

Such careful planning, sensitive execution, and thoughtful followup, should help you and your students carry out meaningful and satisfying service projects.

32

What Have We Learned About Catechesis?

"What I don't understand is what good has come out of all the changes in teaching religion since I learned the Baltimore Catechism. It seems now more and more people want to go back to the way it was then. What have we learned from it all?"

Your question comes just as we are preparing a talk on "Practical Tips from Great American Catechists." We pulled together some of the important, lasting contributions of American catechists during the last fifty years.

Here is our summary. We hope is helpful. In a way it sums up the entire present book.

Content

(a) Teach the traditional Catholic beliefs, prayers, practices and moral norms—all Catholics have a right to know their heritage.

(b) Appeal to people's intellectual capacities, stimulating them to think critically and to question, and helping them to understand.

(c) Have people memorize key aspects of Catholic faith tradition—beliefs, prayers, bible facts and stories, liturgical rituals, important people and events.

(d) Focus on Jesus Christ as the central content of catechesis, helping people to know, love, and follow him.

(e) Aim at touching people's hearts—where the affective content of catechesis is grasped, e.g. trust, love, commitment, joy, peace.

(f) Share the highlights of God's saving intervention into history so people can discover God's constant love for humanity and the world.

(g) Draw continually on the Bible, the liturgy, the witness of saints and other great Christians, as well as Catholic doctrine.

(h) Let your caring example and your way of dealing with those you teach be for them a witnesses of Christ's love.

(i) Listen carefully to your experiences and questions as well as those of your students for echoes of God's Word spoken in daily life.

(j) Value human experience as an integral part of your lessons' content, along with the Bible, liturgy, doctrine, and Christian witness.

Process

(a) Plan your lesson carefully to relate a segment of your students' experience with an aspect of Catholic faith that honestly speaks to that experience.

(b) To facilitate the faith process, keep lesson plans simple, focusing on a single theme, with each step building clearly on what went before and leading to what comes after.

(c) Engage your students in the key learning strategies of reflection, dialogue, prayer and action in relation to life and tradition.

(d) Remember, the catechetical process of consciously relating people's lives with their Catholic tradition—repeated over and over—is more important than any of its parts.

Context

(a) Do all you can to foster an experience of community within you class, faculty and staff.

(b) Make an on-going effort to involve parent(s) and the family community in students' faith growth.

(c) Relate your lessons to events in your local parish and diocese as well as in the national and world Church.

(d) Draw attention to events in your neighborhood, town or city, our nation and foreign countries to foster a sense of participation in the world community.

(e) Help students recognize their responsibility to the broader community, particularly to the poor, weak, hungry, homeless, aged, and victims of war and injustice.

(f) Lead your students in appropriate works of compassion to suffering individuals and works of justice aimed at changing unjust institutions and structures.

Methods

(a) Plan with an eye as much on the learners as on the content—on their experiences, needs, abilities, learning styles, attitudes, questions, and background.

(b) Work at creating a learning environment that stimulates interest, is comfortable and welcoming.

(c) Foster an atmosphere of serious learning balanced with fun.

(d) Use stories: Bible stories, stories from children's literature, stories from personal experience, and stories from the media.

(e) Use music and song often, both religious and popular.

(f) Use poetry regularly, the work of acknowledged poets as well as your own poetry and that of those you catechize.

(g) Use pictures—photos, slides, films and filmstrips, videos, secular art as well as sacred art.

(h) Concentrate on your language—polish it until it is simple, concrete, experiential, and poetic.

(i) Involve learners in activities that creatively engage their imaginations, feelings, and bodies as well as their intellects—drawing, writing, discussing, making things, playing games, role playing, dramatizing, moving, dancing—so they do more than just listen to you.

(j) Make the most of available resources: people, magazines, newspapers and TV, commonplace things, as well as your textbook.

These are some of the valuable things we've learned through the past half century of catechetical development. We have much to be grateful for and many faithful, creative catechists to thank as we continue to explore new catechetical horizons in a changing world and Church.

Bibliography

This brief bibliography highlights *practical* resources for catechists. It does not pretend to be complete, as the books to which it refers give ample listings of many more useful books, as well as media.

Official Church Documents

Vatican Council II: The Conciliar and Postconciliar Documents, ed. Austin Flannery (Costello Publishing, 1987)

Sacred Congregation for the Clergy, *General Catechetical Directory* (United States Catholic Conference, 1971)

National Conference of Catholic Bishops, *Sharing the Light of Faith— National Catechetical Directory for Catholics of the United States* (United States Catholic Conference, 1979)

Pope John Paul II, *Apostolic Exhortation on Catechesis* (United States Catholic Conference, 1979)

Helpful Catechetical Books

Greg Dues, *Teaching Religion with Confidence and Joy* (Twenty-Third Publications, 1988)

Thomas H. Groome, *Christian Religious Education—Sharing Our Story and Vision* (Harper & Row, 1980)

Brennan R. Hill, *Key Dimensions of Religious Education* (St. Mary's Press, 1988)

Janaan Manternach and Carl J. Pfeifer, *Creative Catechist* (Twenty-Third Publications, 1983)

Matias Preiswerk, *Educating in the Living Word* (Orbis Books, 1987)

Thomas P. Walters, *Making a Difference* (Sheed & Ward, 1986)

Periodicals

Catechist (2451 East River Road, Dayton, OH 45439)

The Catechists' Connection (PO Box 419493, Kansas City, MO 64141)

Group's JR. HIGH MINISTRY (Box 407, Mt. Morris, IL 61054)

The Living Light (c/o Department of Education, USCC, 1312 Massachusetts Ave., NW, Washington, DC 20005)

Religion Teacher's Journal (PO Box 180, Mystic, CT 06355)

Today's Catholic Teacher (2451 East River Road, Dayton, OH 45439)